A True Story of Love, Commitment, Courage, and Faith

What Happened to Our Happily Ever After?

When Your Soulmate Dies of Cancer:
Moving Through and Moving On…
Becoming Better, Not Bitter

LINDA CONN ARMENTO

What Happened To Our Happily Ever After?

Copyright © 2024 by Linda Conn Armento

All rights reserved.

Cover art & design © 2024 by Big Giant Media, Inc.

Layout by Big Giant Media, Inc.

Published by **Linda Conn Armento**

lindaconnarmento@gmail.com

First Edition

Published in San Marcos, CA (United States of America)

Published simultaneously worldwide

Identifiers:

ISBN: 979-8-9915761-0-9 (paperback 6x9)

ISBN: 979-8-9915761-1-6 (epub)

Library of Congress Control Number: 2024912808

To Bob

"Those we've held in our arms for awhile,
we hold in our hearts forever."
~Author Unknown

This is a story about a young woman who, at twenty-one years old, assumed she had it all. But, piece by piece, she lost it; the fantasy love story she had always dreamed of slowly but surely disappeared. Yet she managed to survive and thrive.

My goal is to provide encouragement in this life, especially if you think you have reached the end of your rope. I've tied many knots in my rope, and now, approaching seventy, I know I am not finished yet.

My prayer is that this story will give you hope and perseverance to continue on your journey and find your purpose, no matter what may come your way.

Based on a true story…

Some names have been changed for privacy purposes.

Table of Contents

Foreword

Linda Conn Armento has demonstrated a unique ability to pull her readers back to a time and place in her life that set her and her loved ones on an unexpected path with an unknown future. As a result of her lifelong habit of detailed journaling and her exceptional memory, Linda takes her reading audience on an adventure few have experienced at such a young age. At the same time, her memoir offers life lessons learned along the way. This is a book that would surely be enjoyed by young and old alike, a memorable story about love, emotional strength, and most of all human resilience.

~Cindy Crew, Cousin

CHAPTER ONE

Fairy-Tale Princesses
and Other Fantasies

A S I MULL OVER my early childhood days and that infamous princess who ultimately set me up for disappointment, I distinctly remember falling for that compelling fantasy notion…hook, line, and sinker…desiring that life for my own. I dreamed about a handsome prince who would come along and sweep me away, making me the happiest girl in the world. I would live "happily ever after." Ever after what? Oh, how those words stung in my heart twenty years later when I heard them echoing from long ago.

As a young girl, I convinced myself that if I found the right man, the rest of my life would magically fall into place; I would be content and complete. If I set my heart on it, my dreams would come to fruition. One famous princess assured me that a dream is a wish my heart makes. My heart wished for nothing more than to find my prince.

I had done my fair share of dating in high school and kissed enough frogs to know that I would know when I met Mr. Right. I recognized certain traits and personalities that worked for me—and some that did

3

not. And through that process of elimination, I realized early in my life that I was ready to meet the man of my dreams. I was determined.

In the fall of 1972, after graduating from high school in the San Fernando Valley where I grew up, it appeared that might just happen. Maybe, just maybe, those fairy-tale princesses were right after all.

And then it happened. It did! I found my prince. During my first semester of college, I attempted to crash an afternoon health class. There he sat across the room, appearing confident and friendly. A warm feeling came over me. It was desire mixed with attraction, an overwhelming urgency or chemistry. Aside from whatever it was, I knew, without a doubt, that I had to meet this man. Even if we were only to be friends, I needed to know who he was. I was curious to learn more about him. Perhaps I had an intuition.

The instructor took attendance. "Robert?" she called out.

When he responded, I repeated his name in my head: Robert. I wondered if he had a nickname. Rob, Bob, Robbie? There was an air of mystery about this guy, and I wanted to know more. From what I could see, he was tall, handsome, and had a contagious, inviting smile. For some reason, unbeknownst to me, I was intrigued. He had me captivated.

One fairy-tale princess taught me that along with happy little bluebirds, fairy dust, and seven seemingly helpful dwarves, finding the man of my dreams would ensure that I would live the rest of my life in a beautiful dream state, happily ever after. Oddly enough, I knew in my heart, at that very moment, I had found a possible prince, my prince. Now I just needed him to find me!

When the first day of the class ended, the instructor told me I was on the wait list with good potential to enroll in the course. As I was leaving the classroom, I noticed that Robert and I were both nearing the door, so I paused and timed it so he would hold the door for me, allowing us to exit together. It worked!

I smiled shyly at him while his extended arm held the door, then he and I walked side by side along the path toward the parking lot. While we walked, we chatted about the class, and I told him of my dilemma. When we parted ways, he said he hoped we would see each other again the next week.

I returned to class the following Tuesday and found out I was enrolled. Afterward, he approached me, and again we walked to the parking lot together. Bob, his preferred name, rested his keys on top of

Linda and Bob - Early dating days

his classic chocolate-brown 1969 Chevelle, which he was so proud of, and we continued to talk for quite a while. Suddenly, a large black crow flew down and swooped up his keys.

"Hey, you little critter," he called to the bird while running under him through the parking lot. "Bring back my keys!"

We laughed so hard when the bird finally dropped them, and it was evident to me at that moment how easygoing Bob was. Between the twinkle in his beautiful brown eyes and our chat, I recognized that he loved life. He told me he lived in Los Angeles but asked if he could call me sometime and if I would like to go out. So we exchanged phone numbers before leaving for home.

A couple of days later, he called and invited me out. I was thrilled when he took me to an ice cream parlor near our college. Being a typical neurotic, self-conscious teenager, concerned about my weight and what people might think, I ordered a salad. I was trying to impress him and let him know I was on top of my figure. I so wanted him to like me. We chatted for a couple of hours across the booth that evening; Bob was talkative and genuine.

"How did you decide to travel twenty miles to a college in the Valley? Wouldn't it have been easier to stay closer to home in LA?" I was curious.

His reply surprised me.

"I heard there were some pretty cute girls in the Valley, and I wanted to see for myself," he smiled with a sparkle in his eye.

I could feel myself blushing, but at the same time I felt quite lucky that he had made that decision.

As we walked to his car, I thought that regardless of what might develop between us, I hoped we would always be friends. I enjoyed being with him; I felt comfortable and extremely safe. When he dropped me back at my house afterward, he walked me to the door, pulled me into his arms, and gently, tenderly kissed me. My entire body melted with desire for this man. Afterward, I bolted to my bedroom and wrote about our first date in my diary.

After that night, aside from seeing each other in our weekly class, Bob and I enjoyed many long phone conversations, slowly getting to know one another. During that time, I found a suspicious lump in my breast. It felt so natural to share this with Bob. I told him how scared I was, and he assured me he would be there for me, no matter what; and he was attentive with sweet cards and phone calls.

Thankfully, the cyst was benign, but through this process I learned more about his character and what a caring person he was. His support brought us closer, and we were slowly becoming best friends.

A little over a month after we met, Bob brought me a card that read, "Open This Card Only If You Love Me."

Oh my, I could not open it fast enough. Inside, it read, "Thanks. I love you too." Then I found a beautiful love note handwritten to me, telling me he hoped we could continue getting to know one another moving forward in our relationship. It was all happening quickly, yet my heart was in sync with his. We both felt an urgency not to miss an opportunity or waste a moment.

My heart was pounding when I left Bob that day, and I felt

something inside that I had never experienced before. There was something unique about him that was sending exciting messages all through my body. I felt giddy about what was happening. Every love song on the radio suddenly came to life, and I was singing right along when I realized this was just the fantasy my mind had planned. It felt incredible being near him. My heart was dancing all the way home; I was falling in love.

Over the next several months, we spent most of our free time together and eventually met each other's parents, families, and friends. His best friends, Rocky, John, and Marty, welcomed me in, as did his brother, Bill, and his sister, Pat. Over time, he met my cousins, Cindy and Jim, my friends, Cheryl and Wendy, and my sister, Sandy. Everyone supported us.

We were both full-time college students, working part-time, but we managed to squeeze in as much time together as possible. Also, Bob was pledging a fraternity and I was pledging a sorority, which kept us both busy. We had so much in common and loved sharing life. Bob was in an

Wendy and Cheryl with Linda

oceanography class and began taking scuba diving lessons; I studied child psychology and dove into tutoring young children. I loved waiting for him to return from the ocean with his catch of the day, usually abalone, which he would prepare for our dinner.

A favorite memory of mine was at a frat party, safely nestled in Bob's arms, dancing cheek-to-cheek to the Beach Boys singing *Surfer Girl*. I knew then that I was right where I needed to be.

One Saturday, Bob suggested a trip to the LA Zoo with my students, three brothers from Israel. I was thrilled he wanted to do that, and I loved watching him entertain those curious little boys, delighting in showing them all the animals. I could easily imagine what a wonderful father he would one day become.

When our first Easter arrived, we went to church and had breakfast with my grandparents. Later that day, Bob took me to the church where he grew up, was baptized, and served as an altar boy. It was a beautiful structure on Wilshire Boulevard in Los Angeles, and on that late afternoon, when we arrived, we found it locked.

"I think I can figure out a way in, Snookie Bear (our pet name for each other)."

After finding an open window, he climbed in and opened the door for me. We quietly walked hand in hand down the cobblestone aisle toward the magnificent altar; I gazed in awe at the colorful stained glass windows lining the walls. I secretly hoped that I would one day walk down that same aisle in a wedding gown. We knelt at the marble altar and prayed.

"Thank you, God, for bringing us together. Please keep us close to you and to each other, always."

I had never felt as connected to anyone as I did to Bob. My heart filled with joy as we held hands and pledged our love for one another before the Lord, for I was confident I would one day become his wife.

Bob made me feel precious and as though I was the prettiest and most remarkable girl alive. He was always complimentary, telling me how lucky he was to have met me. Recently, his best friend Rocky reminded me of this time, early in my relationship with Bob. He and Bob were driving to the Valley to visit me from Los Angeles, where they both lived at the time.

Rocky recalled telling Bob, "This sure is a long way to drive to see a girl, bro." To which Bob replied, "You haven't met Linda."

Everyone knew we were so in love. Or so I thought.

A couple of months later, Bob called and told me we needed to have a break from one another. Of course, I was devastated and did not know how to move forward. I knew he must have had good reasons, but none made sense. Though I did my best to understand, it was heartbreaking. I would see him across the campus at school, talking to others, and wonder what was going through his mind. Had he met someone else? I quickly eliminated that thought as it was far too painful to ponder.

Two weeks later, Bob finally called me again and explained what was happening.

"My dad has been having seizures, Linda. Last Monday, we found him passed out in his real estate office."

He continued, "Paramedics took him to the hospital where they ran some tests, and we just found out he has a malignant brain tumor." His dad was only forty-six, and we later realized the tumor had metastasized from a previous skin melanoma.

Suddenly, it all made perfect sense. Bob was overwhelmed and needed to be there for his family without distraction. But, at the same time, he was unsure how to tell me. Being the oldest child, he realized the upcoming responsibilities that would fall to him, especially if his dad passed away. Bob was nineteen, confused and overcome by grief, yet his mother, seventeen-year-old brother, and fifteen-year-old sister were relying upon him to be strong. And then there was the family real estate business he now felt obligated to carry on. He had little energy left over for a relationship, yet we slowly drifted back together. As we did, we realized that we were supposed to be connected. We had strength as a couple and supported each other during this agonizing time. I was with Bob in the hospital while we visited his dad. We both learned from that experience that if we were to succeed as a team, we needed to feel safe to share the good and the bad. Together we made that promise.

Vividly, I can recall the final day his dad was on life support; Bob and I were at his bedside along with one of his friends, who invited us for dinner. I felt an urgency to stay, which I later realized was intuition. I urged Bob to do the same, but he needed a break and decided to go with his friend. Alone with Bob's dad in his room in the ICU, I whispered into his ear that I would be there for his family and support Bob in his absence. I strongly, yet softly, heard an inner voice urging me to offer him peace and comfort. Unaware of what I was doing, I realized I had encouraged him to go with God. He died that evening.

My future father-in-law, Jim, was the first person I had ever been with who was close to death, and I learned a valuable lesson that day, one that I would later apply many times throughout my life. I recognized that nothing I could do would help save or fix him, and I somehow knew, in my spirit, he needed peace to pass.

At twenty years old, I knew that this feeling did not come from me. I followed a gut instinct to listen to God and have been forever grateful that I did. That was not the first time I heard from God, nor would it be the last.

I will never forget watching Bob deliver the eulogy for his father in the church where Bob and I had prayed together just one year prior. He stood tall and proud as he described his dad and what he had meant to him. His best friends, Rocky, John, and Marty, were also there. I was so thankful Bob and I had reconnected and were able to walk through that traumatic time together. We grew closer as he sorted

Bob with Rocky and John, circa 1974

through things and decided what to do next. I fondly recall countless hours in coffee shops—planning, discussing, and dreaming about our future together.

Recently I found letters and poems Bob wrote me not long after his dad died. They clearly describe his fears, feelings of depression, inadequacy, and uncertainty about his life as a young man. He expressed how part of him wanted to run away and escape, but the other "stable Bob" wanted to get married and begin his own life. He was scared.

And here was what he wrote to me just a few months before his father passed:

Bob felt the need to continue with the family real estate business, which thwarted his dreams of studying at USC or joining the Navy. His grandmother, Betty, fondly known as "Bopsy", started the company in the 1940s, and his dad joined her soon after he finished college. I don't believe the thought of pursuing real estate appealed to Bob before his dad died, but I knew once he put his mind to it, he would persevere and successfully embrace the challenge.

Real estate classes filled his nights, followed by heavy study sessions in preparation for the sales license exam. During the day, Bob was in the office learning from the other agents, reading notes his dad left behind, gleaning all he could. He was approaching his twentieth birthday with much hope and aspiration for a bright and promising future. He was mature beyond his years.

I continued to flourish, taking more college courses, and eventually accepting a full-time position with a local civil engineering firm. We were growing as individuals and bonding as a couple. Both of us had the highest of hopes for our lives together. And while my dreams of meeting a real-life prince unfolded, I would eventually discover why it felt so urgent.

CHAPTER TWO

And the Two
Shall Become One

"NEVER PUT ALL OF your eggs in one basket," Mom would say.

What a strange statement, I used to think. But the older I became, and hopefully much wiser, I recognized that as great advice. Because—as we all know—most things in life are temporary and can disappear in a heartbeat, sometimes without notice, with the exception of a spiritual belief, which for me is eternal.

But from Mom, I learned to keep my options open.

As a mature teenager approaching the end of high school, I was eager to leave home and enjoy my independence. During a brief discussion with my dad, he curtly said, "Go to the local community college and take typing and shorthand. That will land you a good job, and you'll need nothing more."

"But Dad," I argued, "Cindy and Cheryl are both going to a university. That's what I want to do."

"It's great that your friends are going away to college, but this is all

I'm willing to do for you. And I know you'll be a wonderful secretary."

Alright then. The goal for me was clear. So, what did I do? I promptly signed up for junior college. As it turned out, my dad did me the favor of a lifetime. During my first week of classes, I met the man of my dreams. Now granted, I still had resentment and anger toward my father for his lack of encouragement and support. As a young girl and teenager, I often overheard my father tell my mother, "She will never amount to anything."

Feeling like a loser, I held onto those words deep in my spirit, but outwardly I fought against them. Since the message came from my father, it somehow had to be true. Yet, even though he set limits on my potential, my desires and dreams were still alive deep inside me. No matter how hard he tried, he would not destroy those. I silently promised that to myself, so naturally, it was a fantasy come true when I met Bob.

Raised in a typical 1950s home in suburban Los Angeles, my dad, an engineer, was the breadwinner, and my mother was a stay-at-home mom who loved her children and never pursued anything beyond her high school diploma. Nothing wrong with that. Mom was intelligent, but she became dependent upon my father in many ways. As the years continued, I subconsciously made the decision that would never happen to me.

My dad was quite successful in his field and thus provided a lovely lifestyle for our family. He was committed to his marriage and to his two daughters; he was present in our home and showed us how to be trustworthy, honest, responsible, and dependable. He was a man of integrity, but he was also an authoritarian. At a very young age, I witnessed the power and control a man can have over a family dependent upon him for survival. I learned to fear men, especially my father, and was always aware of the wrath that awaited me if I did anything that was less than perfect.

Yet at that young age, I also had light, love, and hope beginning to seep into my world. With good intentions, beginning when I was about seven, my parents dropped my sister and me off at the local church for Sunday School while they visited a nearby coffee shop. I was learning about a Creator who loved me completely, considered me 'wonderfully made', and would never leave me. Between Sunday School and a grandma who taught me about faith, I knew if anyone could calm me, it was Jesus. So, many nights when I was alone in my bed, feeling frightened and anxious, I prayed and asked him to be with me and protect me.

My father did not hold back on punishments for minimal crimes, often with a flat wooden board on my bare bottom. When he did, it hurt so badly that I cried. He would then glare at me and say, "Stop crying, or I'll give you something to really cry about."

I learned to suck it up, not display my emotions—especially to him—and bury my pain. I then strived to be perfect. And what an IMPOSSIBLE accomplishment that was. I continually beat myself up verbally and felt a deep disappointment whenever I failed. The voices inside my little head were ferocious and taunted me incessantly. And soon, a pattern developed. Whenever life went well, I knew something awful was around the next corner. Continually, I waited to be punished and assured myself that whatever had happened to make me feel that way was most likely my fault. I convinced myself that I had done something to deserve it but was clueless about what I did that was wrong.

As a result of my strict upbringing, I constantly second-guessed my decisions, re-examined conversations with friends and family, and wondered if I had said anything wrong or hurtful.

Relentlessly, I tried my best to be perfect in every way. The mere thought I had hurt or insulted someone—or caused them to think less of me—was more than I could bear. Can you imagine the energy this took out of me? And for what? I was a fearful, insecure young girl with very low self-worth who grew into a young adult who worked hard to find her way. As a teenager, I became borderline anorexic as I tried to maintain a thin body, always seeing myself as overweight—but I was not. Fortunately, I never became out of control in that area, but as I look back, I realize I was trying to take charge of my life. I was also seeking approval and validation, especially from men.

After graduating high school in 1972, I attended a Campus Crusade gathering at a local church. At the end of the meeting, the leader offered a prayer inviting us to pray and ask Jesus to come into our hearts. Combined with earlier childhood experiences, that hit me like a lightning bolt. Without any doubt, I silently prayed the prayer and have not looked back since. It made perfect sense to solidify my walk with God, who would ultimately always love and approve of me.

Soon after, I decided to become a different person than I was throughout my childhood and teen years, because I realized I now had the perfect opportunity to do so. Since I would be with a fresh, new group of students at junior college, most of whom I did not know, I could be whoever I wanted. So I chose confidence and strength, among other positive qualities, and soon walked onto the campus with my head held high while a cloud of freedom enveloped me. And then I met Bob.

Although he emulated many positive traits of my dad, he differed from my father in significant ways. Being with Bob was easy since he was kind, funny, slow to anger, and loved me unconditionally.

Even though that seemed like a new concept...realizing that a man could and would love and treat me respectfully and without judgment, no matter what … it really wasn't. You see, I had the good fortune of growing up down the street from my cousins, Cindy and Rick, and their parents, Aunt Juanita and Uncle Dick.

My Uncle Dick became the man I revered as a male role model.

He displayed traits and qualities that I admired—for one thing, he was easy to talk to and approachable, not scary. He was kind and loving and opposite my dad in so many ways. He was fun to be with!

When I was nine, for example, he took Cindy and me to our local record shop and bought me my first Beatles "45." As we were driving home, he looked at me and chuckled, "Now please don't write me a thank you note for this—I already know you appreciate it!" He was so easygoing.

My uncle loved music—including, but not exclusively, country western. One Friday evening he popped a rock and roll tune on his stereo and taught Cindy and me how to do the 'Twist.' I will never forget that night and how special I felt dancing with him in the living room.

Uncle Dick loved me unconditionally, and he also loved Bob. The two of them were similar and got along great. In fact, when he passed away, my aunt asked Bob to deliver his eulogy. To this day, I believe my uncle was the reason I was first drawn to Bob. I recognized something special and familiar.

So over the next several months after his father passed, Bob and I continued to date exclusively, and I learned more about this man and his incredible qualities, falling more in love with him every day. Getting to know one another during that time, and grieving his father, helped us grow us even closer as a couple. It was clear that God intended for us to be together. We had no doubt.

* * *

"Dear Diary: Bob and I went to the mall today to shop for the perfect wedding rings. After visiting several jewelry stores, we finally found just what we wanted and put down a deposit for both of our rings. We then went to my house, and Bob talked to my dad about marrying me. It was a tense moment for me, but Mom and Dad were thrilled. Today was truly one of the happiest days of my life!"

* * *

On a cold, rainy night in November, a little more than two years after we met, we sat alone in the real estate office, the same office his dad had been in only months before. Bob had purposefully planned to be in this spot to feel his father's presence, which we did. As I curled up in his weathered leather chair, Bob knelt on one knee, took my hands in his, and stared into my eyes.

"I love you so much, Linda. I can't imagine my life without you in it."

My heart was pounding so hard it seemed it would leap out of my chest.

"Will you marry me?" Bob asked, barely above a whisper, while tears pooled in his eyes.

I was thrilled to say yes as he pulled me into his arms and kissed me. Indescribable joy filled me and tears streamed down my cheeks; I was the happiest girl in the world.

His mother and my parents were thrilled when we shared the news. We had everything to look forward to; our lives together were about to begin.

* * *

Two months later, Bob and his friend Marty found Bob's mom unconscious on her bedroom floor. He called me right after calling 911. The ambulance took her to the same hospital where his dad had died just nine months prior.

She remained in a coma for several days until the doctor finally told us she most likely would not recover. Bob notified Reverend D'Amico, who came to give her the last rites. We held her hands, and as he spoke, I watched as tears softly rolled down her cheeks. I knew she could hear us, even as she was in the last moments of her life. Later I learned that hearing is usually the last of our senses to go. Shortly after, Bob had to decide to remove his mom from life support, after which she slipped away from us pretty quickly. She was only fifty. The doctor said her death was due to a heart attack. I still believe it was a broken heart.

In less than one year, Bob and his younger brother and sister had lost both of their parents abruptly and tragically. It was unbelievable how strong Bob was and how he held it together with dignity and grace. It was, however, almost more than any of us could bear. We were now all too acquainted with death and its sting. The realities of life were staring us in the face, and we could not run from them.

The next day, I stood quietly next to Bob while he completed the final arrangements for his mother. Together we selected her clothes, a casket, the music, and scripture. It was all too familiar. And, once again, we returned to the same church and Reverend D'Amico. This time Bob's sixteen-year-old sister gave the eulogy. It was a beautiful tribute to her mother, which she delivered eloquently. It was terribly sad to watch these three young siblings as they grieved the loss of their mother.

After the service, I stood by the casket and stared at his mother, who, in six months, was to have become my mother-in-law. It was surreal to see her lying there wearing a pretty red floral dress with matching red lipstick.

That night, she came to me in a dream. Standing in my bedroom doorway, she appeared as she did in the casket, yet alive and smiling at me. It was as if she were telling me she was fine, and that she was happy Bob and I would be living life together.

Although I never had the privilege of having his folks as my in-laws, I felt blessed to have known them. I was comforted by the dream and eagerly shared it with Bob the next day. We both agreed that she had given us her blessing, which provided peace for us.

The next few months were a blur while Bob prepared for his real estate exam, and together we planned our June wedding. I was on a cloud as the dream of

Bob and Linda~June 21, 1975

becoming his wife was now a reality. And, although Bob was more than knee-deep in responsibility, I knew he was also looking forward to our big day.

Once we were married, we would live in the flat above the real estate

Mom and Dad

office, so we spent our free time looking for second-hand furniture. I fondly remember adoring each treasure we found to furnish our home.

On June 21, 1975, I walked down that cobblestone aisle again, this time to join Bob at the familiar marble altar, where Reverend D'Amico—who had recently officiated at both of Bob's parents'

funerals—now delivered our wedding vows and united us as one.

"Til death do us part," we promised to each other. There were no words to describe the unbelievable feeling I had inside me. Bob WAS the man of my dreams. And, from that day forward, we had our whole lives ahead of us.

Surrounded by friends and family, we celebrated the beginning of our fantasy journey together while we danced cheek-to-cheek to Karen Carpenter singing "We've Only Just Begun." Our childhood best friends were there—Cindy, Sandy, Cheryl, who were my bridesmaids, along with Wendy, Cathy, and Marty. Rocky flew in from Germany, where he was stationed in the Army, and John came from Connecticut. Our joyous reception lasted long into the night as we treasured all the gifts and love given to us, while as we began our lives together as husband and wife. And how we enjoyed the first couple of years of our storybook marriage, full of hope for the future!

As planned, Bob and I moved upstairs from the office into a two-bedroom flat, perfect for a newlywed couple. Bob, at twenty, was the oldest of his siblings and was now head of the family. His younger brother and sister, eighteen and sixteen at the time, depended on us for stability and support but also wanted to give us our time alone. They mostly stayed with family friends, but each intermittently camped out in our guest room when they were in between places. We always looked out for them and made them feel welcome.

One day, shortly after we were married, Bob took me to lunch and asked if I would consider quitting my full-time job and join him in the real estate office. The idea occurred to him when his office manager, who had stayed on after his father passed away, announced her retirement.

"Why would I hire someone else when you are fully capable of handling this position?" he asked.

Of course, I agreed and happily submitted my resignation to the insurance company where I worked on nearby Wilshire Boulevard.

I dove in and learned all about real estate. Bob was so encouraging as I became proficient at escrow coordination, office management, and the organization of staff meetings. Eventually, he nudged me to study for my real estate license, which I did. And soon I passed the exam.

Could I be any happier? I often asked myself. I was not only married to the man of my dreams, living the life I had always hoped for, but I was also working with him full-time. Fortunately, we got along well and our complementary strengths, gifts, and talents made us a strong team in so many ways.

A short time after Bob had taken over the family business, his aunt moved his elderly grandma, Bopsy, back to live with her at her home in Michigan. At eighty-seven years old, Bopsy had lived in the flat next door to the office and downstairs from us, so we saw her often. I grew quite fond of her the more we were together and we always included her in our family gatherings.

When his aunt moved her, it was a shock, but with all that Bob already had on his plate, he just wanted what was best for Bopsy, and we knew we had no choice. We had to let her go. Her care was the priority now, and it was out of our control. Bob was close to his grandma, and keeping her real estate business alive was important to him—and ultimately meant a lot to her.

One day, Jack, one of the long-time agents working in our office, strode in with a copy of the local daily newspaper. He had it opened to the obituary column.

"Look what I just found, Bob," he said, handing him the paper. We stared in shock at a picture of Bopsy, who had passed away in Michigan. To learn this from the newspaper was disturbing, but we suddenly realized the reality of unhealthy family dynamics.

In no way did we deserve this cold notification, but we knew that Bopsy would want us to move on. Undoubtedly, it brought much sadness, but Bopsy had modeled the stamina and perseverance to move forward. She left us with this prayer I found in the office one day and saved. It was what she often used to open her business meetings many years prior:

"Our Heavenly Father,
as we gather here this morning,
help us to be mindful of thy
presence in our daily lives and
grateful for thy many favors to us
all. We thank thee for the privi-
lege of meeting here in the spirit
of cooperation and mutual trust
and friendship. Strengthen and
fortify our will and our ability
to serve well in our work and be
with us and within us in all that
we say and do.

Linda and Bopsy

"We ask thy guidance, thy direction, thy support,
and thy protection for each and every one of us—humbly and
reverently—

"Amen."

This wonderful lady was an inspiration to us and so many others. I was blessed to have known her.

By now, Bob was soaring in his real estate business and was studying to become a broker. He was nominated the youngest President of the Los Feliz/Silverlake Real Estate Broker's Association in Los Angeles. He simultaneously presided over the local Kiwanis Club. His public speaking and ability to engage in conversation with anyone of any age were astounding. At twenty-three years old, Bob was well on his way to success, and I was thrilled to stand by his side and support all of his professional endeavors.

Real estate group installs officers

Robert E. Conn was installed as 1979 president of the Los Feliz/Silver Lake Real Estate Brokers' Association Inc. at Michael's Restaurant, Los Feliz, on Dec. 1.

Other officers installed were John Wilcox, first vice president; Jack Bennett, second vice president; Don Merton, secretary; Sallie Floberg, treasurer; and Mary Frances Hill, executive secretary.

President of Conn Realty Company, Inc., Conn obtained his Real Estate Sales License in April of 1975, following the death of his father, James E. Conn.

Conn Realty Company was started in 1946 by Robert's grandmother, Betty Conn, who later was joined by her son, James E. Conn, both of whom were prominent real estate leaders in the community.

Conn has been an active member of the Los Angeles Board of Realtors and the Los Feliz/Silver Lake Real Estate Brokers' Association since 1975. He obtained his Real Estate Broker's License in July of this year.

He also is a member of the Wilshire Chamber of Commerce and Wilshire Kiwanis Club. Conn is the youngest president in the history of the Los Feliz Brokers' group.

PASSING THE GAVEL — Robert E. Conn, left, newly installed president of The Los Feliz Silverlake Real Estate Brokers' Association, receives the gavel of office from outgoing president William Paul Baltz. Conn was installed, along with the rest of the officers for the coming year, in recent ceremonies at Michael's Restaurant, Los Feliz. (Bob Waits Photo)

I recently found the motto Bob adopted and kept tucked inside his wallet. Bob lived by this standard; it set him apart from others in the real estate industry. This attitude enabled him to succeed while being admired and respected. I couldn't be more proud to be his wife.

*"The Salesman sees a "prospect"—an individual with
whom he may be able to "do business"
and thereby earn a commission.
The Professional sees a "problem"—a "People" problem he may
be able to solve in
the event he and the client decide to work together.
—I'm a Professional—"
~By C. Charles Chatham*

Eventually, Bob and I saved up enough to buy our first house. We found and purchased a new home about thirty miles from our office, and we enjoyed decorating and landscaping our perfect three-bedroom cottage. Bob's sister Patty moved in with us while she started college and navigated that new season of her life. She was now eighteen.

With the real estate market flourishing, we eventually relocated to a larger home in a beautiful avocado grove. Patty moved to a place of her own, while my sister Sandy who was also eighteen, occupied one of our spare bedrooms with her new puppy. We lived there for almost two years. Bob and I celebrated our third anniversary and continued to build many happy memories. We feverishly enjoyed and appreciated our wonderful life, filled with much hope for our future.

CHAPTER THREE

The Missed Diagnosis

O UR THIRD YEAR OF marriage came with some unexpected challenges, beginning with Bob experiencing some abnormal bleeding. Being so young, we assumed it was probably a benign issue but wisely decided to contact a doctor. Since Bob was only twenty-three, it was not an immediate concern, so a routine exam was scheduled. But with all we had experienced recently with his parents, we had a different attitude and were determined to stay on top of our health issues and beat the odds.

"You have hemorrhoids," the doctor told Bob. He prescribed medication and sent us on our way. We felt relief and certainty that his diagnosis was nothing of concern.

Feeling like the issue was resolved, Bob and I were becoming anxious to start our family. For several months, I took my daily temperature to pinpoint my ovulation. Since we worked together in our real estate office, we had a lot of flexibility and fun with the timing of ovulation day, which was never dull. But after many attempts to get pregnant, we began to think we might need some assistance.

We soon ventured into the unknown world of infertility. I will never forget driving alone down the I-5 freeway in Los Angeles to meet my love for dinner. My period had arrived once again, that morning, and I was having another of my many conversations with God. That time we were discussing the potential infertility diagnosis.

"If infertility is our battle and what we are to contend with, I can do that, God." After all, I already had been given an unbelievable relationship. So if that was what we had to deal with, so be it. My inner voice reminded me that having children with Bob would be a bonus because my magical life with him was already more than any girl could ever hope for.

Life was about to become a little more stressful when we visited my ob-gyn, Dr. Brooks, who determined that we both needed to schedule an infertility workup. That was just the beginning of multiple tests and doctor appointments, which would consume our lives in more ways than we realized. He told us the first part of the workup was the sperm test and handed Bob an instruction sheet, which we took to the lab. Never would I forget that day.

We were heading to San Francisco for a weekend getaway, but since the lab was on the way to the airport, we decided to stop by. When we checked in, the girl at the desk asked Bob if he had his sperm sample with him.

A surprised look came over him as he told her he was unaware he was supposed to provide one. She then handed him a small jar and another set of instructions and told him to bring it to the next appointment.

Not wanting to lose more time, Bob leaned over the counter and said, barely above a whisper, "Excuse me? Could you tell me where your restroom is?"

I sat there mortified as he strolled down the hall with his little jar. Shortly after, he returned to the front desk with the filled jar and handed it to a different girl, who asked when the specimen was collected.

"What time is it right now?" Bob replied, grinning.

Her eyes widened, but she fixed her gaze on the jar of warm semen as she recorded the information while I worked hard to keep a straight face. Imagine!

Laughing hysterically, we hurried out of the lab, hand in hand, and headed to the airport. Part of me could not believe Bob had done that, but another part was not surprised. Bob was a realist. He knew it would be difficult for us to wait longer than necessary to find out why we weren't getting pregnant. He liked to "git'er" done with no time to waste. And his sense of humor never ceased to help us through.

A week or so later, we sat across the desk from Dr. Brooks and listened while he explained that Bob's sperm count was low; it was, in fact, almost non-existent. And the amount that he did have had very slow motility. In other words, it would be a miracle for us to become pregnant without tremendous help, but we were willing to do whatever it took, no matter what. Dr. Brooks described the next part of the workup and what we would do afterward. It was my turn to undergo tests. We left his office feeling disappointed, but at the same time hopeful.

Bob and I decided to explore a different way to expand our family. After much searching, we found the cutest little beagle puppy, brought her home, and named her Brandie. She was amusing and quite entertaining and was the perfect distraction for us during that time of infertility. Brandie was indeed our new baby.

When my father-in-law was alive, he had a special friend, Ray, who was also one of his longtime clients. After Bob died, Ray took us under his wing and mentored Bob as he began his real estate career. Ray had moved from Los Angeles to North San Diego County and would often invite us to visit him and his wife there. As he showed us around the county, we became enamored with the up-and-coming area and thought it would be a great place to raise our family. We both wished we could eventually relocate, but the family business in Los Angeles held us back. We spent much time dreaming and brainstorming about how we could pull it off.

We continued to commute thirty miles while working in Los Angeles but began to notice changes in the neighborhood. First, we heard about a girl being raped outside the YMCA two doors down. Next, a robber held up one of our salespeople at gunpoint in the rear parking area of our building. Fortunately, he was all right, but as a result, we began locking our doors during business hours to keep track of who we were letting in. When left alone in the office, I naturally had a lot of anxiety and fear.

Finally, one morning, as Bob and I pulled up to our office to begin our day, we noticed a bullet hole through the double fluorescent sign in the front of our building—the sign that Bob had built and installed himself when he took over the company. We looked at each other in horror and agreed that we didn't want to die in the heart of Los Angeles. We both had learned firsthand that life was short and oh-so uncertain. It was as if we were receiving a sign from above that it was okay to end that chapter and do what was best for us. As we drove home that day, a song from the 60s by The Animals popped into my head. We laughed and sang, "We Gotta Get Outta This Place," feeling thankful for the epiphany. It was amazing how God showed us the way out.

Over the next few months, we determined what to do with the business, listed our house for sale, and strategically planned our move south. This decision was, of course, an emotional one, but we were more than ready.

After much planning and hard work, we sold our home in the avocado grove and hired a manager for our real estate business. Those decisions made it possible for Bob and I, along with our beagle pup, Brandie, to relocate from Los Angeles to the dream home we found in beautiful Carlsbad. At that same time, I was undergoing further testing for infertility, as we were nearing two years of unsuccessful attempts to get pregnant on our own.

Recently, I found a card Bob wrote to me shortly after the extensive workup at UCLA Medical Center. On the cover of the card was a simple staircase, showing a beagle dog who had crawled to the top and was on his belly, barely able to see the bone in his view, just inches away from his twitching nose. The card read: "You made it! Congratulations, Mrs. Guini Pig! Love, Mr. Guini Pig." He went on to say, "Dear Snookies, I am really sorry you had to go through all that prodding, pushing, and checking, but now, like the little beagle on the front of this card, victory is just on the next step! Thank you for being so patient about all this stuff. It sure is a strain for anyone to go through all we have for what is so easy for everyone else. But, I will say one thing; we are both drawn closer together as we try! I sure do love you, Linda, and I thank God we are lucky enough to have each other. I pray nothing more serious than this ever comes our way! I LOVE YOU!! Bob - Mr. Guini Pig"

This card was dated May 29, 1979, just a couple of weeks before our lives were about to change forever. Yet Bob had unwavering hope.

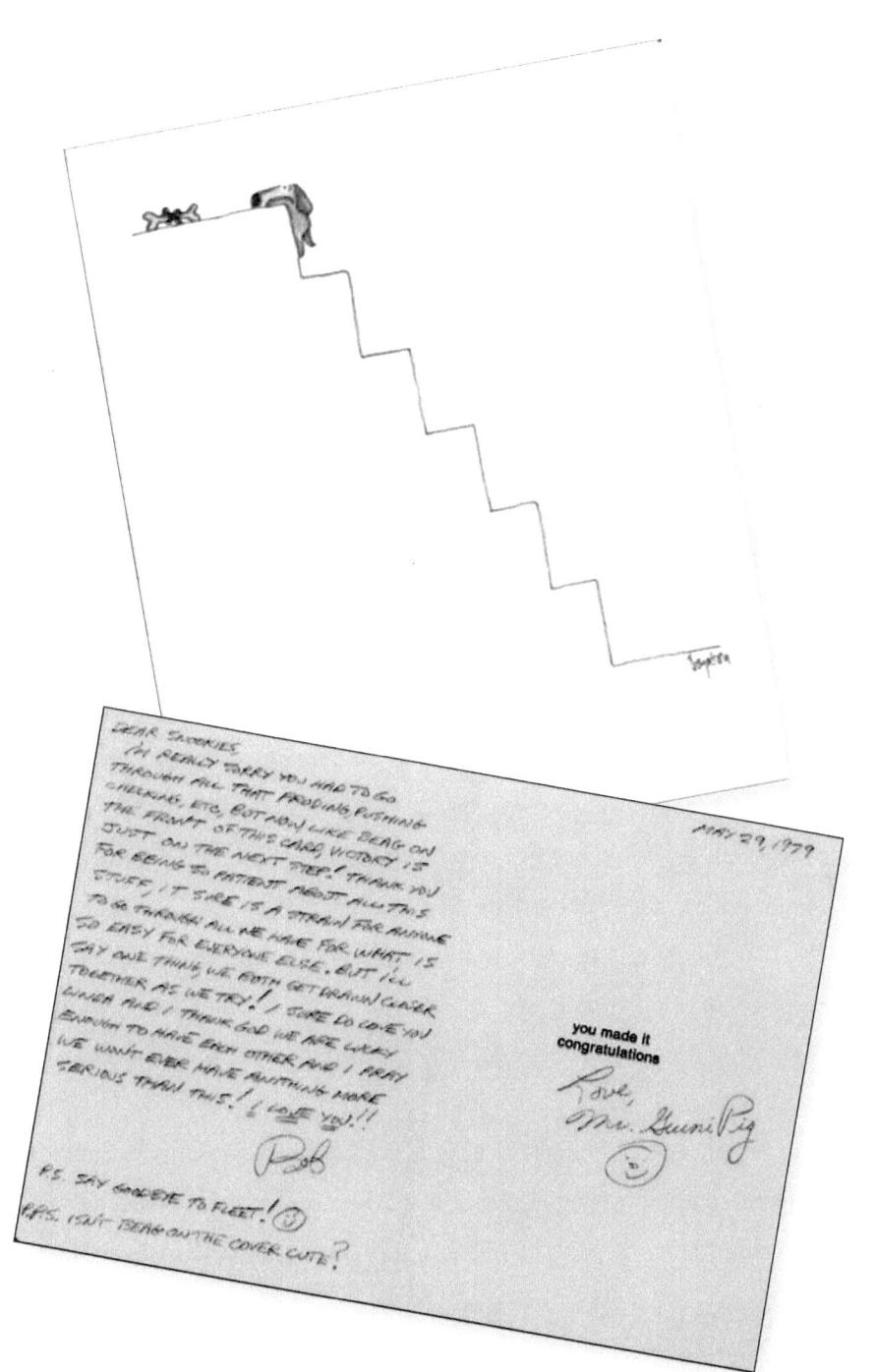

DEAR SNOOKIES
I'M REALLY SORRY YOU HAD TO GO
THROUGH ALL THAT PRODDING PUSHING
CHECKING, ETC, BUT NOW LIKE BEAG ON
THE FRONT OF THIS CARD, VICTORY IS
JUST ON THE NEXT STEP! THANK YOU
FOR BEING SO PATIENT ABOUT ALL THIS
STUFF, IT SURE IS A STRAIN FOR ANYONE
TO GO THROUGH ALL WE HAVE FOR WHAT IS
SO EASY FOR EVERYONE ELSE. BUT I'LL
SAY ONE THING, WE BOTH GET DRAWN CLOSER
TOGETHER AS WE TRY! , I SURE DO LOVE YOU
LINDA AND I THINK GOD WE ARE LUCKY
ENOUGH TO HAVE EACH OTHER AND I PRAY
WE WON'T EVER HAVE ANYTHING MORE
SERIOUS THAN THIS! (I LOVE YOU!!

Bob

P.S. SAY GOODBYE TO FLEET! :)
P.P.S. ISN'T BEAG ON THE COVER CUTE?

MAY 29, 1979

you made it
congratulations

Love,
Mr. Guini Pig
:)

33

CHAPTER FOUR

The Real Diagnosis

B OB WAS AN OLD soul and lived his life with passion. Among other things, he taught me to live in the moment and that relationships were, by far, the most valuable part of life. He treasured the people in his life, and it was evident.

One morning while we were getting ready for our day, sharing hugs and kisses, he suddenly gripped my shoulders and, with an endearing glance, warned me not to get too close to him. He stated that he was pretty sure he would not live to be very old. He reminded me that since his grandfather and father had died in their forties, why would he not feel that way? I was shocked to hear him say that and asked him to stop talking like that. It made me feel sad and scared. I immediately pushed that thought down deep inside, not realizing it would one day return to haunt me.

"I had a terrible night last night, Linda," Bob said one morning, a week or so after moving into our new home in Carlsbad. "I had a lot of bleeding, so I'm guessing I'll need surgery on those darn hemorrhoids of mine."

Without hesitation, I pulled out our local yellow pages and searched for the closest doctor in our new, unexplored neighborhood. I found a nearby gastroenterologist and quickly called for an appointment. When I told the receptionist that his main symptom was rectal bleeding, she booked an examination for us that afternoon.

We both wondered what was involved in hemorrhoid surgery on our way to see the new doctor.

I sat in the waiting area while Bob went in for the exam. Not long after, he returned, and I could tell immediately by the paleness and look of fear on his face that something was wrong. He sat down and quietly said, "The doctor scoped me, Linda, and found a tumor which he said didn't look good."

We held onto each other as we sat silently in the waiting room. I fought to hide my fear and angst. I knew I needed to be strong right then.

Soon the doctor invited both of us in and made it clear that he wanted Bob to undergo a lower gastrointestinal (GI) test to rule out more tumors, followed by a biopsy of the one he had just discovered. Obediently and much like robots, we went to the local drugstore to purchase the items necessary to prepare for the lower GI. Bob needed to have his intestines cleaned to detect any other tumors. We were about to embark upon the beginning of critical changes that would ultimately alter both of our lives.

The next day we were ready. Bob and I went to the hospital for him to undergo the lower GI test. He was in great spirits, especially considering what he had been through the day and night before. After the test, his intestines were full of barium fluid, so Bob bolted to the nearest restroom and found it locked. He sprinted down another hall and made it just in time. Bob came out with his trademark smile, and as we left the hospital, he chuckled, happy to be done with the procedure.

The following day we returned to the hospital for the tumor biopsy. We knew it had to be a bit serious to be scheduled on a Saturday, but we were also thankful to put it behind us. It was then that the first of many waiting games began. Yet during this time, Bob remained hopeful and optimistic, and somehow, was able to maintain his sense of humor, which was so much a part of who he was; always smiling and comforting others around him. That is not to say that he wasn't worried. He was. We both were. We were twenty-four-year-old newlyweds, launching a new business, moving into a new home, and anticipating becoming parents. How could this be happening to us? And, what if the rarest of rare diagnoses did happen? What then?

The Fourth of July was just days away, and our families and close friends came to visit: Rocky and his girlfriend, Esther; my folks; cousins Cindy and Jim, and their baby girl, Katrina, just six months old; our friend Ray; my sister Sandy; and Bob's brother and sister, Bill and Patty. They all came to support us. We strived to keep a positive attitude, but the knot in my stomach continued to grow. Yet I tried hard to stay in the present and not think too far ahead. After all, Bob was young, and we knew that even if this were something serious, we had caught it early enough, and he would be fine. But it was hard not to think, worry, and ponder the what-ifs swirling around in our heads.

"We will take care of this bump in the road, put it behind us, and move on with our lives," we continually pledged to one another. That became our constant prayer.

> *"Life is not about waiting for storms to pass.*
> *It is about learning to dance in the rain."*
> *~Vivian Greene*

Amid a storm, you may want to run away and head for shelter and safety. Some life tsunamis, however, cannot be escaped. They undeniably must be endured.

The thorough pushing and prodding pelvic exam I encountered a few weeks earlier revealed that I was as fertile as possible, so it was time for the next step: artificial insemination.

We were entering the third year of our attempt to have a baby and were pursuing the next part of the process. After carefully evaluating my monthly cycle and confirming the perfect timing, I drove to the fertility department at UCLA Medical Center with my little jar of semen, which we had collected together. As I lay on the icy cold metal examination table, I prayed for success, that we would finally hear that we were pregnant. Although this procedure was not how I had envisioned getting pregnant, I realized we were blessed to have options. And since it was so very clinical, I assured Bob I was okay to go alone. It was a painless, relatively quick procedure, and I just longed to put it behind us and move forward.

When the process was complete, the doctor advised me to remain calm and unemotional to improve our chances of success. He said I needed to go home, rest, relax, and eliminate all stress or worries.

Meanwhile, Bob was helping pack up an elderly couple who were the last tenants left in our building, bringing us one step closer to ending our ties in Los Angeles. As I drove over to pick him up and head back to our Carlsbad oasis, my excitement was soaring at the thought of the results this procedure might ultimately bring. My hopes were high, even though the past two years had been full of disappointments, month after month. We were supposed to live happily ever after—why was that so difficult?

When I arrived, Bob was almost done and was visibly pleased to see me. I was pretty sure he noticed the glow of joy on my face. I went inside to get him a drink of water, and while in the office, the shrill clanging of the landline stopped me. I assumed it might be a friend or family member looking for us.

But when I answered, the voice on the other end identified himself as the doctor who had examined Bob the week before. I felt a deep chill race down my spine, and my legs buckled beneath me as I reached for the nearest chair to collapse.

My stomach began to form that oh-so-familiar knot of fear, and adrenaline raced through my veins while I listened to him share what no one ever wants to hear.

"I am so sorry to tell you this, Linda, but the tumor we found is malignant and has possibly spread, although we must operate to confirm that. Bob needs to get his affairs in order this week and meet with a surgeon to schedule surgery for next week. You will need to relay all of this to him. Again, I am so sorry."

"Okay," I whispered but barely heard myself speak. In a state of shock, I took down the name and number of the surgeon we were to contact, and as we said goodbye, I put the phone down and sat frozen like a statue, numb with fear and angst.

What was happening? How could this be my life? It must belong to someone else.

Slowly, though, it all began to sink in. The dreaded possibility Bob and I were most afraid to hear was now a reality. Bob had cancer. I hung my head and wondered how I would tell him this news. But I knew I had to. And that was only the beginning of difficult situations and conversations brewing ahead. I needed to be strong; for him, if for no other reason.

So, I took a deep breath, asked God for strength, and went back outside to Bob, who was still loading boxes onto the truck. I walked over toward him and motioned to a couple of chairs in the pile of furniture. I asked him to sit with me as I handed him a cup of water. He was glad for the break.

There was no need to beat around the bush, I thought. It was better to get it out in the open and move on with what was next to come. I knew that would be how my husband would prefer to handle it. So I took his hand in mine, looked into his sparkly brown eyes, and told him that the doctor had just called.

"The tumor is malignant, Bob, and he wants us to meet with a surgeon as soon as possible."

His facial expression did not show surprise, and I imagined deep down inside he already knew.

Calmly, he took me into his arms and assured me we would get through this together. Although I was comforted by his reaction, I still felt scared. So many unknowns loomed before us. My young mind was spinning.

Bob loaded the last few boxes just as the movers arrived to finish the job. Back together in our car, he drove us home to our haven in Carlsbad while we both attempted to sort out and absorb the recent news and tried hard not to think too far ahead. So much for the advice the UCLA doctor had suggested. It was suddenly impossible to eliminate stress and worry as a deep sigh escaped me.

I held tightly to his hand, closed my eyes, and silently prayed to make it through whatever was to come next. I fought hard to suppress the tears pooling in my eyes. We were so far from the fairy-tale fantasy I had wished for—what was happening to our dream?

True to form, Bob was the strong one.

"We will get through this, Snookie Bear," he said softly, his arm tightly around my shoulders. I melted into him and immediately felt his strength and positive attitude envelop me. Eventually, I began to calm down while the burning tears I had held back streamed slowly down my cheeks. His optimistic outlook was our anchor, as well as his incredible sense of humor. He never lost hope.

CHAPTER FIVE

Finding the Right Surgeon

O H LORD, HELP US, I thought while sitting across the desk from that first surgeon in nearby Encinitas. We were there to hear details of the recent tests Bob had endured and what the prognosis might be.

Our hands entwined as we listened openly to his speculation about the probable outcome after surgery.

"First of all," he said, "there is a possibility that we could lose your rectum since the tumor is located so low in the colon, and that could quite possibly result in a colostomy," he began.

"But a new device has been invented, which, when inserted into the rectum, sutures it on the inside. If successful, this will reconnect that part of the colon once the tumor is gone. Having tried it on laboratory animals, I am eager to use it on a patient, a human being."

"As I studied your films, I realized that we probably won't be able to contain all of the tumor and cancer cells that have most likely spread."

The knot in my stomach burned as we grasped each other's hands tighter and listened to this grim report. I could not begin to imagine what Bob was thinking or feeling. The surgeon continued as if we could bear to hear more.

"There will most likely be radiation therapy prescribed post-surgery to eradicate any cancer cells remaining in your body. Unfortunately, this treatment will very likely leave you sterile, Bob."

Since we had done everything possible to conceive, this was the final hit to implode our dreams. Unless our recent attempt at insemination was successful, our dreams of having a baby anytime soon had become smashed to bits. But having a baby was not our focus at that moment in time. Compared to what we were learning, the infertility issue suddenly became insignificant.

Bob and I sat together in a state of shock, and it took all I had to hide the look of fear that was quickly welling up inside me. I willed myself to hold back the tears stinging in my eyes. I knew I had to wait until we were alone.

Be strong, Linda, I silently told myself. Bob needs your support right now, and you need to listen, ask the right questions, and be present.

After a long pause, the surgeon inhaled deeply, looked at me, and asked if he could speak to Bob alone. Bob and I, totally unsure of what we were dealing with here, glanced at each other with looks of terror as I stood up to step out of the room. I could not imagine what he had yet to tell Bob, but after listening to the previous conversation, something in my gut told me this was not the right doctor.

While adrenaline rushed through my veins, I flew down the nearest staircase and grabbed hold of the payphone in the lobby. With trembling hands, I quickly dialed my best friend from first grade. Cheryl was an RN at Cedars-Sinai Medical Center in Los Angeles, where her grandmother had recently recovered from colon cancer.

"Cheryl, I need the number of the surgeon who operated on Grandma Toots," I cried into the phone. "Bob has been diagnosed with a malignant tumor and needs surgery soon. It doesn't sound good."

Cheryl immediately gave me Dr. Sherman's number in Beverly Hills, and when we hung up, I called his office and made an appointment for the end of the week. My twenty-something-year-old intuition told me we needed a second opinion.

Just then, Bob stepped off the nearby elevator; he looked devastated. I slipped my hand in his while we walked silently to the car. As we sat together, he told me that the surgeon had further explained that the tumor was in a delicate area. Therefore, the nerve controlling his ability to have an erection could potentially be severed. The surgeon went on to tell Bob that if that did happen, there was a pump he could use to correct it, or he might want to consider an implant.

We held onto each other while we both cried. So much information had come at us so quickly that we could barely catch our breath before the next bit of bad news hit. We clung tightly to each other in silence and tried to absorb all we had just learned. I then shared my conversation with Cheryl and the upcoming appointment in Los Angeles, attempting to give him a little hope.

"This is not the only doctor we can go to," I softly told him. "We need to get another opinion. We are in this together, Bob, and together we will beat it." I was searching for hope.

We then headed back home to our safety zone and, after dinner, snuggled up in a tight hug. While we tried to escape the millions of thoughts swirling around in our heads, we fell asleep.

At the end of the week, we arrived on time for our appointment in Beverly Hills. The office was lovely, delightfully decorated with antiques and old-fashioned comfort. We sat together, my hand firmly in his, and waited. Meanwhile, I tried hard to keep my fear and anxiety in check, and I prayed for a positive attitude and a better outcome than the first surgeon had offered. I knew it could never be as awful as the previous appointment. That was a disaster.

"Bob?" the nurse called.

We followed her down the hall to a beautiful office, where Dr. Sherman greeted us from behind his desk. As he rose to shake our hands, I felt an indescribable peace inside.

"Have you lost weight recently, Bob?" he asked.

Immediately I knew we were in the right place. While Bob explained that he had previously been on a diet to lose a few pounds, he had reached a comfortable weight and was happy with the results. It was apparent that Dr. Sherman recognized something else.

As we began to discuss the test results, Bob and I requested that he include both of us with anything he had to say.

"We are in this together and we don't want any secrets."

He was very agreeable to that arrangement.

Next, we discussed the surgery that needed to happen soon. Dr. Sherman described the procedure and how he would do it. As he spoke, we anxiously mentioned the stapling device the previous surgeon had told us about, wondering if he had heard of it. We told him that he had used it on laboratory animals but had felt confident that it might save his rectum.

"Oh yes," Dr. Sherman said. "I was involved in the invention of that device. I have used it on many people, quite successfully."

My body immediately relaxed, and visibly, I could tell Bob, too, was at ease. We smiled at one another and squeezed hands; we knew we were in the right place.

We continued to discuss the other possible side effects of the surgery, including the potential loss of the ability to obtain an erection.

Dr. Sherman had much more confidence that this was not a concern. Bob and I again grinned at one another; we knew this second opinion was invaluable.

He then instructed us to go home, get our affairs in order, and have Bob check into nearby Cedars-Sinai Hospital in one week to prepare for surgery.

We drove to our dwelling of security, our paradise. The place where we could go and attempt to pretend that everything was normal—that all of those other horrible issues we were trying to cope with were non-existent. It continued to be our refuge of hope.

CHAPTER SIX

The First Surgery

***

B OB LOVED HIS GREEN surgical scrubs. He had found them for a
Halloween party a few years back when I dressed as a nurse, and they
helped him feel somewhat detached when he wore them in the hospital.
Perhaps they gave him a different perspective than that of a patient. For
that, I was glad. He needed any distraction he could get. And oh, how he
used those scrubs to their full potential.

On the eve of his first surgery, July 19, 1979, I crawled into his
hospital bed and sat with him. Dr. Sherman had advised us to write our
wills. I remember thinking to myself, What are we doing? We are in our
twenties. This is crazy.

But we wanted to do the right thing, so we put pen to paper and
created our wills. Bob's goal was to protect me financially, so he clearly
stated that if he died during surgery, I would receive all we had built
during our short life together. It felt so foreign to be doing that; it was
unnatural and almost self-sabotaging. But we did it because we knew we
had to. There was simply no other choice.

Afterward, we looked at each other, both realizing that it might
be the last night Bob could perform naturally. It seemed important to
capture that moment.

"Let's do this," he grinned.

He closed the door to our private hospital room and probably put a Do Not Disturb Sign on the door. Or, knowing Bob, he may have previously alerted the nurses not to come in, totally embarrassing me.

We then enjoyed what we prayed would not be our last time making love the usual way. Bob, in his scrubs, made it all the more exciting as we both pretended we were sneaking a private moment—he as the surgeon, and me the lucky recipient—while we knew that anyone could walk in at any given time. There were no locks on the hospital doors, but we agreed that we did not care. It was about us, and we intended to live in that moment and enjoy it to the fullest. I worked hard on controlling my thoughts and staying focused on what we had on that given day. Tomorrow could very well be different, but today was ours. We needed to do this, NOW! So, we did. And we enjoyed each other to the fullest.

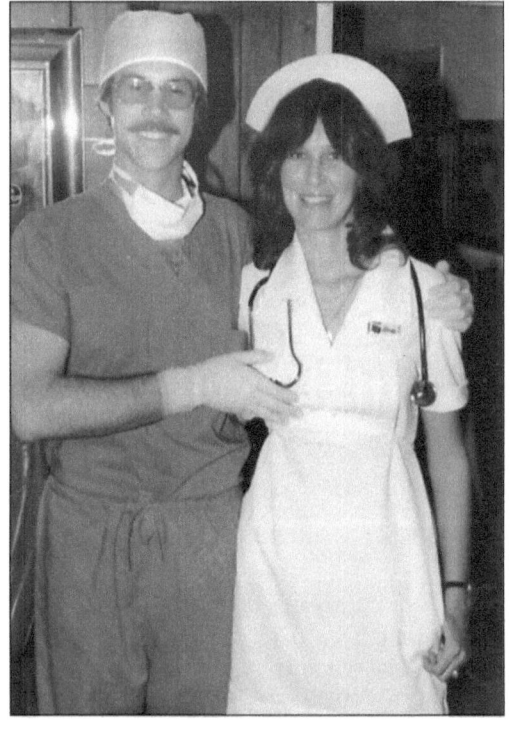

I had to admit that I experienced numerous emotions during our time together. The good girl in me was afraid of getting caught. But I reminded myself that I was married, for goodness sake. Still, I would have been horrified if someone had walked in on us. I also had a raging fear about what that moment of making love represented.

Yet, I pulled myself together and enjoyed our intimate moment in that scary hospital bed, making love with my husband, who had much more courage than I did. He had to face the next day, the lengthy surgery, and all of the unknowns. What a lot for a young man to absorb, fathom, and endure. Yet, true to form, he did so with dignity.

Retreating to my cot afterward, just below his bed, we both attempted to fall asleep while feeling utterly satisfied physically and spiritually since we had connected as one. But emotionally, I was filled with perpetual anxiety and sadness, which loomed over me as I thought about Bob undergoing the dreaded surgery.

And as I lay there wide awake, I allowed myself to wrestle with the many thoughts going through my mind. Then, I tried to imagine the emotions that Bob felt. Quietly I wept, even though I tried so hard not to. Bob was quite stoic about it all, and although he remained positive and strong, he had his limits.

A few days before we went to the hospital, he said, "Linda, if I have to have a colostomy and become impotent and sterile as a result of this cancer, I would rather be dead." And that was not to mention the ever-looming thought of having cancer and the treatments yet to come. That was a hard one to talk him through. But I did; I talked him off the ledge, and he ultimately chose to go through with the surgery.

Finally, after much prayer, my mind shut down, and I drifted off to sleep, listening to him breathing softly above me. I knew I needed to be fresh and ready for the following morning. Bob was counting on me.

We awoke early and attempted to prepare for the unknowns we had yet to face. It was a Friday morning, July 20, 1979. At 6:00 a.m., Dr. Sherman came by our room to check on us, and we were both in the restroom. While I grabbed a quick shower, Bob, who had just dried off, was blow-drying his hair.

He knocked on the door. "Good morning, guys. I will see you downstairs in the surgical ward."

A wave of adrenaline rushed through my body.

Soon the gurney rolled in. Bob had previously been prepped and was ready for surgery. I held onto his hand and walked alongside him as we wheeled into the elevator that took us downstairs to the surgical suite. The gurney paused at the large double doors, which opened into the sterile, brightly lit room, just long enough for me to kiss Bob goodbye, to tell him I loved him, and to assure him I would be there waiting when it was over. He was brave as he smiled at me from the gurney and said, "We can do this, Snookie Bear." I smiled, blew him another kiss, and held back my tears until he was behind closed doors.

Briskly, I walked past my family in the waiting area and ducked into the restroom, where I cried, prayed, and got my period. Instantly, I glanced upward inside the bathroom stall. Okay, God, I whispered. I get it. I surrender. You are in control, not me. It is your way, not mine. Despite feeling sad and disappointed, I felt the freedom of resignation. I was weary from trying so hard to be strong, and I appreciated the opportunity to relinquish my desire for control. At that moment, I realized I was powerless and desperately needed something or someone to cling to for reassurance that I would make it through. I knew in my spirit that God was all I had to lean on right then. Bob was my earthly pillar, but God was my never-ending support and guiding light, my constant and unwavering rock. Everything and everyone else somehow suddenly seemed so temporary to me.

I wept while I prayed for God to give me strength. I knew that when Bob came out of recovery, whatever that outcome was, I would also have to share this news with him. Our valiant efforts to become pregnant—

exactly two weeks before his surgery—were in vain. I needed to acknowledge the fact that a baby was not in our immediate future. There were more important things that needed our attention. God knew best.

But, at twenty-four that was hard to accept. It was all so confusing and discouraging. And not what my fairy-tale dreams had promised me. I returned to the waiting area where my family and close friends sat and began the long vigil. The doctor said it would be at least eight hours before he finished. That Friday proved to be one of the longest days of my life.

After a couple of hours passed, a young man walked into the waiting area carrying a bouquet of one dozen beautiful red roses. He asked if Linda Conn were there. I looked up and realized they were for me. Tears sprang to my eyes once again as I read the attached card:

"Linda:
Thank you for making this seem more like a circumcision
than what it really is.
I love you.
Bob"

I was shocked, as was everyone else in the waiting room. Who does that?! But it was not unlike Bob to step out of himself and think about me. He knew how hard this was for me, and he acknowledged that. I suddenly realized, for Bob it was never about him. He embraced the situation with dignity and class and always thought more about how it affected others than himself.

As the day slowly moved forward, the end finally came. Nine grueling hours later, the surgeon walked through the double doors, into the waiting area, and approached me. I recall two portions of our conversation; one I heard, and the other I chose not to. As time passed, I recognized I had used my selective hearing while he spoke. I heard him say that he had surgically removed the tumor, but he recommended radiation just to be sure. He assured me that the operation went better than expected and that Bob would be okay. He was able to reconnect the colon, so there was no colostomy. And he was pretty convinced that the one critical nerve was not damaged. Bob would stay in the ICU for four days before returning to his room on the seventh floor on Monday.

Most of that was true, but the part I left out, refused to hear, or allow into my brain, was that the radiation would be an attempt at zapping the cancer cells that possibly remained or had spread. I subconsciously ignored that fact and reassured myself that we were home free. My interpretation of what I thought I heard was that there was no more cancer, and after the radiation treatments, life would go on as we knew it. We would strive to move forward in our lives, careers, and plans for a family. Oh, how I would live to regret those assumptions.

With the surgery behind us, we came to the end of a long, difficult day. Bob was feeling groggy and needed to sleep, but eventually I was allowed to see him in the recovery room. He would soon transfer to ICU, where I could return the next day to visit him.

Since staying with Bob in the ICU was not allowed, I went home with my cousins, Cindy and Jim, who lived nearby, to get some rest, before returning to our regular room on the seventh floor on Monday.

That night during dinner, I was beaming and told them, "I feel like we just changed the ending to the movie *Love Story*." Once again, my selective hearing was alive and well. But I was not about to give up hope, no matter what.

CHAPTER SEVEN

Come Monday

A S I DROVE BACK to the hospital early the next morning, Saturday, I sang "Come Monday" along with Jimmy Buffett, the song streaming loudly from the cassette player in my car. As he sang about his lonely days in the brown LA haze, I couldn't get back to Bob's side fast enough.

Before his surgery, I stayed in the hospital room with Bob around the clock, but the ICU was different. I could visit but not spend the night. I knew, come Monday, we would be back together again for another week of recovery before we headed home. I would be back on my cot next to his bed. We were in this together. No matter what.

When I arrived in ICU, Bob was wide awake, wondering where I had been and asking where his glasses were. Although I was thrilled to see how well he looked—alert, and sitting up in bed—I was unprepared for this drastic improvement from the previous evening. Bob was in full bloom and was already making significant progress.

"Now, check this out," as he lifted the sheet and pointed downward. In that instant, we both realized that the dreaded fear that the nerve was severed was not even a remote concern. Bob was alive and well. I was thrilled to be a part of that discovery and embraced him in excitement as a big smile brightened his face.

He gleefully explained that there was no colostomy, and he described the incision across his abdomen as "no big deal."

"We can do this, Snookie Bear," he said, as he gently took my hand.

The relief I felt for him was indescribable. I hadn't realized until that moment how much I had been holding inside emotionally, as I was concerned the cancer had spread, not to mention the other possible side effects. My whole body relaxed with a big sigh. I knew, however, deep in my spirit that, regardless of all of this good news, I needed to remain strong, hopeful, and supportive.

Once again, as God had reminded me the previous day when I realized our insemination was unsuccessful, I knew I was not in control. I was so hopeful, though, seeing how quickly Bob had bounced back. In fact, he was doing so well, he was returned to his room on the seventh floor that day. We were back together again for another week while he recovered.

During the next few days, as Bob continued to improve, I eventually found the courage to tell him about our unsuccessful endeavor with artificial insemination two weeks prior.

When we finally had a quiet moment to discuss it, it seemed that we both were so caught up in his recent surgery that having a baby became a back-burner issue, at least for the time being. We were both so disappointed but still very determined, as it gave us hope for the future, and we happily agreed we would continue trying on our own. We also decided to explore the possibility of adoption once we were back home and settled.

Bob maintained his sense of humor and positive attitude while we finished our last week in the hospital. Friends and family visited often, and the nurses on the floor loved him. He was always up to something to keep them laughing.

For example, the day before his surgery, he was wheeled to another floor for a pre-op x-ray. While he lay on the gurney, waiting for his turn, he took an opportunity, when no one was looking, to pull the white sheet atop him up over his head, covering his face. He stayed very still and held his breath, hoping someone would notice. I could only imagine the silent chuckles inside him when the orderlies began whispering about how this corpse just appeared in the hallway. When he relayed the story to me, he laughed so hard at how rattled they were when he suddenly pulled the sheet from his face. He loved playing tricks.

And then there was the time, shortly after surgery, when his favorite nurse walked past his door.

"Oh Helen?" Bob called out from his hospital bed. "Do you still need this urine sample from me?" He was holding up a full urine container, sporting a big smile, with a twinkle in his eye, indicating that he was up to something.

Bob was a trickster, always anxious to make someone laugh, especially during his arduous hospital stays. Earlier that day, he had provided a urine sample to a nurse but somehow ended up with a second empty container, into which he promptly poured some leftover apple juice.

"No, Mr. Bob, I already have one from you," Helen called from the doorway.

"Okay then," Bob replied as he unscrewed the lid and poured the golden liquid down his throat.

Helen screamed, "Omigosh!" as she ran down the hall to tell the other nurses what he had done.

"Got her good," Bob said, smiling at me with that grin I will never forget.

As I rode downstairs to get a coffee, I chuckled about my husband

and his humor. Even during the most difficult of trials, he was a rascal. God bless him.

While in the elevator, I ran into a lady bitterly complaining about the hospital food. She was a woman much older than myself, possibly by two generations, and she was very angry about the meals her husband received following his recent heart attack. I had several floors to ride with her before arriving at the cafeteria, so I stayed quiet while she continued her rant.

She rambled on and on about the terrible food while I listened intently. She finally asked why I was here at the hospital.

"My husband has colon cancer. He is not yet able to eat the food offered here," I replied, trying not to sound bitter or sarcastic. She was suddenly silent, but her eyes showed embarrassment and sorrow.

That time in the elevator was a valuable lesson for me. It taught me to be careful with my words and judgment since I never knew what another person might be experiencing.

Ultimately, however, this woman gave me hope that one day soon, my husband would enjoy the terrible food at that hospital. I could hardly wait.

CHAPTER EIGHT

Back Home in Carlsbad, the Journey Continues

IT WAS AS IF bells and whistles went off early on the morning of July 27, 1979, when Bob received approval for discharge from his room on the seventh floor. For what seemed like months, instead of the two weeks that we had been there, we were anxious to return to our nest in Carlsbad, not to mention our rambunctious beagle, Brandie.

When the nurse eventually brought us the discharge papers, Bob had already ditched the surgical scrubs and traded them for corduroy shorts, a flashy Hawaiian shirt, and flip-flops. Like a convict released back into society, he could not escape soon enough.

"I can't wait for us to break out of here, Linda. It's been too long, and I am sick of this hospital life."

The only change from the hospital scene Bob had experienced in the last two weeks was when he was finally able to eat real food and the doc permitted him to ride down the elevator seven floors to visit the hospital cafeteria. They served the best french fries there, and Bob and I shared a booth and a large order. We smothered them in ketchup and salt and enjoyed each one like caviar.

"Oh Snookie Bear, the little things mean so much, right?" Bob laughed as he finished up the last of the fries. "Who would ever have thought a plate of french fries could bring so much joy?"

The sun shone brightly on the rooftop parking lot as we loaded our luggage. Bob claimed shotgun position, and we thankfully left our Los Angeles quarters.

"Woooo Hooooo!" we hollered as we circled and screeched down level after level of the parking garage. "We are outta here!"

Bob rolled down his window, opened the sunroof, and popped a cassette in the player. Soon we were both singing along to Neil Diamond and his greatest hits.

"How about we grab Brandie and hit the beach!" His face lit up as he poked his head out the window to feel the warm breeze on his face, his brown hair flowing in the wind. He was ecstatic to be in his street clothes, outdoors in the sunshine, and headed for home.

As we cruised south on I-405, Bob reached over and gently took my hand.

"I could never have done this without you, Snookie Bear."

I briefly diverted my eyes from the road, smiled at him, and squeezed his hand. Tears spilled down his cheeks as his hand tightly gripped mine, and I, too, let loose of my emotions. Together we purged the myriad of trials endured over the past few weeks. I realized we both had held a lot inside trying to make it through, but the feelings finally surfaced and slowly trickled out.

I mustered everything inside me to produce a positive and confident voice to convince Bob he would be okay.

"We have made it this far, and we will get to the other side of this, my love," I reassured him. "It will all be all right. And remember, we are in this together, no matter what."

The next few miles were quiet, both of us absorbed in our thoughts. It was challenging to jump off the recent emotional roller coaster and bask in the peace and freedom that now enveloped us. And, deep down, I still felt fear in my gut every time I thought about what we had already endured, let alone what the future had in store. I immediately shoved those thoughts aside and focused on the more exciting things ahead.

"What do you want to do when we get home, besides play with Brandie?" I broke the silence in an attempt to lighten the moment.

"Well," Bob smiled, "first of all, I want to spend time alone with you in our backyard with a glass of wine at sunset and watch Brandie tear around. And we need to start getting bids for our pool and have our fence approved. We have so much to catch up on."

While Bob was in the hospital, I had picked up some magazines, and we had eagerly planned the landscaping for our new front and back yards. After studying many pool designs, we agreed on a black bottom lap pool and jacuzzi. We knew that would entice us to exercise plus provide a fun atmosphere when friends and family visited. So, once settled back in our home, I flipped through the local yellow pages and made some appointments to get a few bids.

Meanwhile, the fence plans needed approval by the builder, as the rules and regulations were quite strict. Since we had an ocean view, we wanted to capture it as much as possible. So, we designed a low block wall topped with wrought iron that would not obstruct our vista of beautiful sunsets over the water. We then made an appointment and headed to San Diego to meet with the builder's project superintendent. He looked over the carefully prepared plans and readily approved them. While we were there, I felt a prompting.

"Are you by any chance hiring?" I asked rather impulsively.

"Well, that all depends. Tell me about your background."

"I have administrative experience with a civil engineering firm, hold an active real estate sales license, am quite familiar with the escrow process from beginning to end, and recently managed a real estate company in Los Angeles."

"Let me introduce you to our office manager," he said quickly.

He led me down the hall to another office while Bob winked at me and returned to the reception area.

When I shared my qualifications with the manager, he told me their escrow coordinator for new home development, Diana, needed to take a leave of absence for breast cancer surgery. They were looking for someone to fill in temporarily while she was out.

After he reviewed my application, he immediately offered me the position. Elated and somewhat surprised, I could not wait to tell Bob. I then informed the office manager that I could not start for about one month. The reason was that Bob needed to have radiation therapy, which I did not disclose, as he and I had made a pact to limit the sharing of this information.

Coincidentally, the course of radiation treatments timed perfectly with the time Diana would be gone for her surgery, so it all fell smoothly into place. Although this was a temporary position, they assured me it would probably lead to more permanent status, including medical benefits. We were ecstatic.

"That could not have gone any better, Snookie Bear," Bob said on our drive home. "I am so impressed that you had the nerve to ask, and they offered you the job. That makes me so proud of you."

I was pretty taken aback myself and still in a bit of shock. Never had I been hired on the spot like that. And adding in this new income, we would qualify for a second loan on our home to afford the new pool. I often wondered, what if I hadn't inquired?

"So many good things are happening for us," Bob said. "How about we plan a party to celebrate and thank everyone who helped us through."

I was never one to turn down an opportunity to be with friends.

"What a great idea! I'll make a few phone calls tonight and let everyone know. Now, what about food?"

"I vote for barbecued burgers and hotdogs," Bob smiled, "and your mom's famous potato salad is always a hit. Oh, and your grandma makes the best apple pie. Everyone loves that."

"I'll see if they can bring it in person," I smiled. It was refreshing to watch Bob happily settling back into his element, living life. He was due to begin radiation therapy the next week, so we were eager to be with our loved ones before he surrendered to the upcoming side effects.

Laughter and music filled our barren back yard the following weekend as we celebrated life on that warm summer day.

"Cheers, everyone!" Bob said, his arm resting on my shoulders, lifting his can of Miller Lite.

"We could never have done this without all of you by our side. Here's to health, happiness, and all the right decisions," he continued. That became his toast at our many celebrations during the months ahead.

Monday morning began the grueling process of radiation therapy, which we had decided to have done back at Cedars-Sinai in Los Angeles. Even though we had the

Dinner with cousins Cindy, Jim, and Rick

option for Bob to go closer to home, we knew the care and outcome there would be the best for him. Besides, they were familiar with Bob, not to mention his surgeon, Dr. Sherman, who was nearby, and we figured that the four-week regimen would pass by quickly. We were determined to have as few regrets as possible when treating his illness.

We arrived early on that first day since the radiologist needed to examine him to determine where to place the tattooed dot that identified the precise location the therapy would be most effective. The five-minute treatments were daily, Monday through Friday, totaling twenty-one days. It was a lot of driving back and forth, but we stayed a night here and there with family or friends to break it up.

On the final day, Bob insisted that we pick up several boxes of See's Candy for all of the folks in the radiology department who had made it so easy for us, despite the discomfort.

"We're going to miss you all, but so glad this is over," he said, smiling at one of the technicians as he handed her a pound of chocolates.

Bob had already experienced some side effects, including hair loss on his abdomen where the radiation was focused, as well as severe burning of the skin in the same area, which was quite irritating and painful. But, ultimately, he was just happy to put it all behind us.

After stopping off at the coast for a celebratory cocktail, it was early evening when we finally returned home. There we found our good friend Ray sitting on our doorstep.

"Hey Ray," Bob smiled, giving him a huge hug. "It's so good to see you."

"Well, well, well," he greeted us. "Finally, you came home. How was your time in Los Angeles?"

"We made it through, Ray," Bob said, "and it was pretty uneventful this time. I am more than ready to get back to work."

We went inside and continued to banter back and forth while I made some dinner. Bob enjoyed his time with Ray and constantly gleaned wisdom from him.

"Well, what's next for you, my friend?" Ray asked.

"I'm looking into a local real estate company to hang my license and get started here in North County. I found a great setup in Leucadia right near the beach. It is a growing firm with many active agents and is the next best thing to owning my own. There's a monthly rent for office desk space and phones, but I keep 100% of the commission on any sales I generate. How can you beat that?"

"I know about that company, Bob, and I've heard good things. It sounds like a win-win," Ray encouraged him.

I put dinner on the table, and we raised our glasses in celebration. Once again, Bob toasted, "Here's to health, happiness, and all the right decisions. Cheers to all of us!" Life was good.

As planned, Bob met with the local broker the next week and signed up with his company while I began my new job twenty minutes south in San Diego. We were suddenly back on the fast track, living as a happy, 'normal' young couple. We spent the evenings and weekends settling into our home, decorating and landscaping. Groundbreaking for the

pool was in full swing, and there was always a project to keep us busy. We planted flowers; Brandie dug them up. We rewarded ourselves by cooking dinner together or exploring all

Fun times in our pool

the fun restaurants in our new area. Local happy hours were our favorites.

One evening in September, we received a call with good news from his best friend, Rocky.

"I asked Esther to marry me, bro, and she said yes!"

Bob immediately invited them down from Los Angeles for the weekend, and we put together an intimate engagement party, just the four of us, during which they asked Bob and me to be their best man and matron of honor. We were so excited for them and could not wait for their wedding day the following February.

Engagement celebration for Rocky and Esther

Bob was finally feeling better and almost back to his old self. We both glowed like newlyweds and had the whole world ahead of us as we celebrated holidays and every day, for that matter. We spent lots of time with friends and family, which was extremely important to both of us. We were very close and were fighting this cancer together. Cindy, Jim, Rocky, and Esther came down frequently on the weekends, and we all embraced the time together as we savored the good times of life. My sister, parents, and Bob's siblings also visited often; we maintained a tight connection.

We were making new friends but kept our secret carefully guarded. "No one needs to know about my cancer, Snookie Bear," he had told me in the hospital. "If they found out, they would not want to do business with me for fear I might not be around long."

Perhaps his dad had instilled this in Bob years prior, but discretion about cancer was a definite issue during that era. I loyally honored his request, even though, as time went on, it became increasingly difficult to do so.

Soon, the big day arrived for Rocky and Esther, and we all celebrated to the hilt. I was thrilled to dance with the man of my dreams while we welcomed Esther into our 'family' and rejoiced in their happiness. We were all very close. Bob and Rocky met when they were only eight and had been lifelong friends.

"I couldn't have made it through this without you, bro," I overheard Bob tell Rocky as the two embraced. "And I'm so happy you found such a great girl. Married life is the best!"

Shortly after the wedding, the forewarned side effects of radiation therapy slowly crept in. Bob was frequently tired, and it became difficult for him to retain any food or liquid. As a result, he was rapidly losing weight.

Celebrating Rocky and Esther, February 1980

I grudgingly got up in the morning after a long night with Bob sick, left him asleep in our bed, and raced to work. Since there were no cell phones, I would call our landline to check on him as soon as I arrived. Whether or not he answered could be good or bad news. If Bob picked up the call, it was good that he answered, but not good that he was still home and not feeling well enough to go to work. On the other hand, if he did not answer, it could be good that he might be out and about working, but then again, not so good because something might have happened that prevented him from answering the phone. Those were difficult times, as I strived to keep it to myself at work. Most of the time, my high anxiety was for naught, and he was usually okay. Once again, I knew I needed to let go and trust God.

When Bob did feel well enough to go to work, he was in and out of the office and frequently in the field, checking out various properties. He often joked that he was familiar with, and had frequented most of the public restrooms and construction porta-potties in North San Diego County.

When the month of May arrived, Bob was extremely weak, as he had lost a total of fifty pounds. After a long month of discomfort and pain, the doctor concluded that there was a blockage. He had hoped it would resolve itself without another operation, but unfortunately, things had not improved. Bob needed relief. They scheduled a second surgery for June 9, also my mom's birthday.

I requested vacation time from work, which was approved. As we headed to the hospital, we wondered what the blockage might be. We spent the long drive up to Los Angeles pondering the unknowns, trying not to go too far ahead in our thoughts.

When we checked in, Dr. Sherman met us in our hospital room. "I'm hoping the blockage is scar tissue in the small intestine from the massive amount of radiation you received, Bob. But the other possibility could be a recurrence of the tumor. Unfortunately, we will not know for sure until I go in and have a look."

Once again, that familiar knot developed in my stomach, that burning pang of fear, but the rest of me, the outside, hopefully, appeared calm. After all, I had to be. I could not let any negative thoughts permeate Bob's positive ones. As much as I silently tried to prepare myself for either scenario, I continued to trust that God was ultimately in control. He had already proven that to me so many times prior.

When we were alone in our room that evening, I snuggled close to Bob. Softly, I whispered, "Are you scared, Snookie?"

"A little, I guess, but I believe this is nothing to worry about," he reassured me. "We've already been through the hard stuff; this is just another bump in the road we'll put behind us."

His outward calmness overwhelmed me in contrast to the turmoil that continued to churn inside me. No matter how hard I tried to push away the scary thoughts, they continued to creep in. But I dared not bring up the what-ifs because I had learned we had no power over what happened. All we had to count on was this moment.

We sat together in his bed and watched a movie, passing the time till morning. Bob was in a lot of pain when we arrived but soon received some medicine, which seemed to keep it under control.

Early the next day, Bob was on the gurney and again passed through the double doors to the surgical suite while I waited outside with our faithful posse of family and friends. Nothing compared to the last surgery, I thought to myself, but I suppose desensitization was setting in. I was still emotional but also a bit numb or guarded. Perhaps that was how I managed to hold it all together. But I also trusted God would keep me centered with his unwavering strength.

True to form, a floral delivery arrived in the waiting area, but instead of one bouquet, it was two dozen red roses; one for me, and one for my mom, for her birthday. Bob was in sheer misery when we arrived at the hospital but somehow contacted the florist before he went under for the second operation. Oh, how my heart filled with gratitude that this man was in my life.

However, when I glanced at Mom and saw tears in her eyes, I knew she was beside herself with appreciation mixed with fear for her daughter and 'son'. I moved closer and held her in my arms while she quietly wept.

"It's going to be okay, Mom," I promised her. "Bob is tough; he will make it through this."

And sure enough, Bob came out of that second surgery with flying colors. The blockage was scar tissue, so the surgeon rerouted his small intestine. After recovery, he returned to his room on the seventh floor, where we spent the next week of our so-called vacation together. We were worn out from the day and gratefully fell asleep while holding hands. He was in his hospital bed while I lay nearby on my little cot.

So thankful for this outcome, we once again vowed to enjoy every minute of life, no matter how hard it might sometimes be. We went home the following week and happily returned to our lives, pressing forward with promising aspirations.

Since Bob had lost a considerable amount of small intestine, where vitamin B-12 is absorbed, it became necessary to supplement.

We visited the doctor to pick up the prescription and discovered it was via an injection into his upper thigh. I learned how to give him the injections, practicing several times on an orange before I felt comfortable giving it to Bob. This new skill was helpful and would prove even more valuable in days to come.

* * *

Early in our relationship, Bob and I had become good friends with the couple who lived across the street from his childhood home. They were much older than us, and both were in poor health. They had adopted a little boy, Barry, who was seven. He was an only child, and we noticed he spent most of his time alone. We became fond of Barry and began to spend time with him, especially when his parents were having a tough day. We loved taking him to the zoo and occasionally for an ice cream cone. At times we pondered what it would be like to adopt Barry if something happened to his parents. Although nothing further developed between us, I often thought about him and how easily we grew to love him.

Little did we know that Barry had prepared us for the next part of our journey; Bob and I decided to pursue adoption.

* * *

As soon as he was feeling better, we stopped by the county office in San Diego, completed our application, and gazed through the photo album of young children needing a home. Pictures of newborn infants, sweet toddlers, and kids of all ages filled us with hope.

"Look at all these precious children just waiting to be part of a family. We have so much love to give, Bob. It seems like this is the perfect solution for us. We will be the best mommy and daddy ever."

Excited for our first home visit a couple of weeks later, Bob and I worked hard to make everything look perfect. We bathed Brandie and bribed her with a bone to keep her calm. We had what it took to provide a loving, happy home for a little one, but for some reason, I felt anxious.

When the social worker arrived with our file, we sat in the living room to discuss the details. While reviewing our application, which included our medical history, she glanced at Bob.

"I see you have a history of cancer," she said. "When were you first diagnosed?"

"It was last summer," Bob told her. "June of 1979."

"I'm so sorry to tell you this, but, unfortunately, you're not eligible to pursue adoption until you've been six years cancer free. We'll put your file on hold for now and reopen it when that status has been achieved. Again, I am so sorry."

That familiar disappointment came rushing in. We looked at each other in dismay as sadness filled our hearts and tears welled in our eyes. But we pulled it together just long enough to say goodbye.

Afterward, I bolted to our bedroom while Bob followed and gently held me. We tightly embraced each other and realized this was another closed door for us; adoption was not an option. Our only solace was knowing we could continue to try to get pregnant naturally. And thankfully, we had Brandie—our happy little family.

"We will get through this hurdle, Snookie Bear. We just have to keep trying on our own," he said, his eyes filled with sadness.

I knew he was right, but deep down, I found it challenging to squelch my pain and focus on the positive. The disappointment of another broken dream was unbearable. Suddenly everyone around me was either pregnant or pushing a stroller. Yet I knew I needed to shove those feelings out of my mind so I could focus on our future together. After all, the last surgery was successful, and we had our whole lives ahead of us. Although our 'happily ever after' had taken a few hits, we both knew there was another plan for the two of us.

Summer approached, and Bob and I often took a happy hour picnic to the beach after work. I enjoyed lying in the bend of his arm, my head resting on his bare, warm chest.

While we sat and enjoyed another beautiful sunset, Brandie ran in and out of the water. I feel so safe, I thought, yet also afraid. I was scared that something worse might happen but smothered those feelings as quickly as they came into my head. Suddenly, Bob pulled me into his arms and kissed me. He knew I was feeling anxious, and he probably was as well. We clung tightly to one another for what seemed like an eternity.

It was too frightening to think beyond that moment. I had invested my heart and soul in this man, and the thought of him not being there with me was terrifying. Yet those fears needed to be thwarted before they overpowered me. If I truly believed God was in control, and not myself, I had to let go of those fright-filled feelings and learn to trust. That was much easier said than done, however.

We were in this together, yet my heart became more fragile as Bob grew weaker. But, I refused to believe that we would not get through this. There was nothing more I could do except enjoy the time we had today.

When I awoke one Saturday morning, Bob was not next to me. I tentatively wandered into the kitchen and found him enjoying his cup of coffee. As I kissed the top of his head, I noticed the travel section of the newspaper and the yellow pages opened to airlines.

"Whatcha doin'?" I asked as I walked over to grab a cup of coffee.

"I'm thinking you and I should go to Hawaii!" Bob smiled as I sat down to join him.

"There are some good deals here, and I think we could swing it. We sure do deserve a vacation, right?"

"Omigosh, I so agree!" I squealed, surprised he felt up to it. "When do you want to go?" I threw my arms around his shoulders and nuzzled my face in his warm neck.

"I would rather go sooner than later and finish this summer with a celebration. We need to make some reservations."

A few months before Bob was diagnosed, we visited Waikiki Beach in Oahu for a real estate seminar and both agreed we would return one day and explore the other islands.

Before we knew it, we had finalized the plane trip and hotel plans. All we had left to do was pack and find someone to watch Brandie. Even though last-minute tickets cost more, our recent experiences taught us that life is uncertain, and this trip was necessary and well-earned. We were aloha-bound!

Our time on the island of Maui was beyond incredible. We filled our days and evenings with sunshine, fresh ocean air, and Mai-Tais. Our love could not have been stronger.

One morning we took a side trip to nearby Kauai and signed up for a boat tour on the Wailua River. The tour included a visit to the famous Fern Grotto, the most romantic spot on the island. We hiked through the tropical forest and came upon a magical spot where we renewed our wedding vows, Hawaiian style. Together, we created a most incredible memory just after our fifth anniversary.

"I love you so much," Bob said one lazy afternoon as we relaxed on the warm sand. I was in my safe spot on his chest.

"I love you too, Snookie Bear," I said as he gently kissed me. "We are one strong team, Bob. I can't imagine my life without you."

I then glanced at the long scar across his abdomen, and reality again set in. We were in the midst of a battle out of our control and were desperately clinging to life.

Summer came to an end with mixed emotions. My best friend Cheryl married Brian, and Bob and I had a wonderful time celebrating their special day. The four of us had become quite close, especially during our hospital stays, where Cheryl worked as a nurse. We could not have done it without her.

After enduring the challenging surgery that summer, Bob and I enjoyed some sweet times together. We strived to move forward in our young lives, hoping that the dark times were behind us and that Bob would begin to feel better and regain his strength in the coming months.

Dancing at Cheryl & Brian's Wedding

CHAPTER NINE

The Third and Final Surgery

I T WAS EASTER SUNDAY, 1981, and our situation was quite distressful. For several months, Bob had been experiencing more than his usual pain. The discomfort was primarily in his abdomen and lower back, but on that particular day, he struggled with unbearable, agonizing digestive issues.

Late in the morning while lying on our bed, he was trying every imaginable position to get comfortable.

"What is happening here? Why are we suffering like this?" I said out loud. We began discussing what was happening and wondering where God was. I pulled out my Bible and searched for a verse that might give us comfort or a sense that God had our backs.

Our faith was strong, but on that particular day we were having doubts. Maybe it was due to our weariness from all we had already endured, especially Bob, or perhaps it was because it was Easter, and we were being reminded of the hereafter and wondering what that meant. I read a few verses aloud and prayed that his pain would subside.

Please let this be temporary, I silently prayed. After all, how much more could Bob tolerate?

Much to our dismay, the pain did not lessen. Instead, it grew worse.

Once again, Bob needed some relief. When I finally reached Dr. Sherman, he recommended an emergency colostomy. At first, Bob was reluctant, but as the pain and discomfort increased, we realized something had to change sooner rather than later. Even though he was quite resistant to the idea, he soon relented as it was the only solution that would ultimately enable him to feel somewhat normal again. And Dr. Sherman had told us that the procedure could be temporary. Little did we know what temporary meant.

So, at the end of May 1981, we returned to Cedars-Sinai for Bob to undergo the much-dreaded colostomy surgery. We waited as long as we could to drive from our paradise in Carlsbad to the hospital, as we knew from much prior experience we would be there longer than we planned anyway.

It was a nice surprise when my dad met us at the hospital that evening. The surgery would take place the following morning.

Bob tolerated the operation, a much shorter one than his previous surgeries. Once again, I sat in that familiar waiting room, anticipating the prognosis. When Dr. Sherman finished and came out to see me, he said it had been successful, given the circumstances, and would temporarily relieve Bob of the pain he had valiantly endured. I exhaled a sigh of relief, yet I knew this would probably be challenging for him.

Bob was sitting up in his bed when the nurse finally led me into the recovery room.

"You look great," I said as I bent down to kiss him. "How are you feeling, sweetheart?"

"Better than I thought I would," while he lifted the sheet and glanced up at me. "We can do this, right?"

I smiled and nodded in agreement. "You bet we can!" I quickly assured him. I laced my fingers into his and softly kissed the back of his hand.

While Bob recuperated in the hospital over the next week and a half, we received training so the two of us would know how to care for and manage this new appliance.

One day, a delightful and courageous young man visited us to provide support and encouragement.

"I had an irritable bowel issue," he explained, "and needed to have the same type of procedure you just had. I finally relented to that dreadful surgery to get some physical relief."

"My wife, at the time," he continued, "found it difficult to cope with how my body now functioned and unfortunately ended up leaving me." He was coping with this condition alone.

Bob looked over at me with terror in his eyes. I grasped his hand, assured him I would NEVER leave him, and reaffirmed that we were together in this. No matter what, I promised.

So that I could be home with Bob full-time, I had quit my job, and since I did not tell them why I needed a leave of absence, they denied me sabbatical pay, disability, or unemployment. Bob needed me at home, and there was nowhere I would rather be. It was the only sensible thing to do, and I had to carefully manage our funds to ensure we could make ends meet. Before quitting, we had taken out a third mortgage to have some money to live on, which provided much-needed peace of mind.

While Bob rested one afternoon, I briefly left the hospital to get some fresh air and take a walk to a nearby bank to juggle funds. As I strolled along the busy street, I lapsed into my head to try and get a mental and emotional grip on what was happening. While deep in my thoughts, the sound of horns honking snapped me back into reality; I realized I was aimlessly walking down the middle of San Vicente Boulevard. For a fleeting moment, I did not care. I wanted to die. I was too scared to face what was possibly ahead.

But, somehow, I returned to my senses and moved over to the sidewalk, which slowly led me back to our room on the seventh floor, where Bob was recovering. He needs me, I told myself. And besides, our sixth wedding anniversary was coming up the next month, and we needed to celebrate.

Meanwhile, because Bob was so weak and tired and trying to wrap his mind around this new way of life, we posted a sign on our hospital door asking friends and family to please understand that we did not want any visitors.

"I just need some time to deal with this and am not up to seeing anyone right now," he told me. That was unlike Bob, who was always gracious, open, and welcoming to anyone who came to see him.

"Have you seen my wedding ring lately, Snookie Bear," he asked one evening. He usually wore it when we went to the hospital.

"No, sweetie. I wonder if we left it at home?"

"I'm not sure. I haven't seen it in a while and have a strange feeling I might have cast it into the ocean that day your Papa and I went surf fishing."

He had lost so much weight that it was no surprise that the ring could have slid right off of his thin finger as he let go of the line. And since he was left-handed, that made perfect sense. Nonetheless, this upset him terribly.

Our original wedding rings meant a lot to us, so Bob was determined to get a new one and have it blessed by Reverend D'Amico, who had married us only six years prior. Since our anniversary was the following month, we decided to celebrate with a renewal of our wedding vows.

It was finally time to leave the hospital and return to Carlsbad and our little Brandie. Our neighbors were watching her, and the minute we saw her, we realized she was in heat. Meanwhile, all the local male dogs were hopping over our fence to accommodate her.

Eventually, and despite all that we already had going on, we took her in to be spayed, which was quite emotional, especially for me.

Bob and I drove her to the vet hospital, and when she returned home, she became another patient of mine. Later, we learned that she had been pregnant, which was almost more than I could bear.

Bob was slowly becoming weaker, but together we nursed Brandie through this. And Bob was, as I had previously predicted, a great daddy.

Brandie continued to be quite protective of Bob. She was his buddy and lay next to him wherever he was resting. Many nights when his pain was out of control, I would play soothing songs on the keyboard, and Brandie and I would sing together. Brandie, being the little hound dog she was, howled to the moon, both of us trying so hard to comfort Bob, calm him down, and for the most part, distract him. Bob loved our concerts!

We also spent a lot of time, mostly at night when the pain seemed to be at its worst, trying hypnosis, a technique we had learned many years prior for relaxation, to get his pain under control. I tried to soothe him when the pain medication was ineffective and we had no other options to relieve him. My pain management skills were less than amateur, and I felt helpless watching my husband suffer. I was now giving him round-the-clock heavy-duty pain injections, but they were not lasting long enough to provide adequate relief. And then there was also the fear of giving him too much, possibly causing an overdose. It was, no doubt, a stressful situation.

Other times, when the pain became unbearable, we used some marijuana his brother had bought for us. Smoking a little weed relaxed Bob and alleviated some of his intense pain and nausea, increased his appetite, and ultimately helped him sleep better. As hard as I tried to convince the doctor, it was nearly impossible to obtain medicinal marijuana during those days. So, we had to be satisfied with whatever we could get.

A week before our upcoming anniversary, we discussed the possibility of buying a water bed to see if that would be more comfortable, especially for his back, where his pain was the worst. We decided to try one out before we bought it, so I made a reservation at a hotel across from the harbor in San Diego that had water beds in the rooms. It was June 14, 1981, when we packed up and traveled south to spend the night.

We had a nice dinner near Sea World at our favorite restaurant, The Atlantis, although Bob was hurting the whole time and ate very little. We went back to the hotel to sleep, but as much as I had hoped this would be more comfortable for him, it was not. He was miserable. I made a mental note to scratch the water bed idea as we drove home the next day. Ultimately, we tried everything we could imagine to provide comfort and relief from the relentless pain. But it now appeared to be spreading to his bones.

The day of our sixth wedding anniversary arrived on June 21, 1981. It was warm and sunny as we drove to the church on Wilshire Boulevard in Los Angeles. Our cousins Cindy and Jim, my sister Sandy and her boyfriend, a good friend of Bob, joined us in celebration. Bob and I had shopped for the perfect outfits for our second wedding attire, and I decided to carry a single red rose. We also found a beautiful new ring for him; gold nuggets sprinkled with tiny diamonds. When we arrived at the church, I had to give Bob a healthy injection of pain medication after the long car ride so he could endure the ceremony. Standing was becoming increasingly difficult for him.

With his new ring in my hand, we again stood at the familiar marble altar, where we had been only six years prior, as Reverend D'Amico reiterated our wedding vows. With joined hands, we again promised: "to love one another in sickness, and in health, till death do us part." That

final vow triggered tears for both of us while I gently slipped the new ring on his finger. It was the most tender, poignant moment, and I fell more in love with him than ever. But the reality of our situation was catching up with me, and it may have been with him also. However, neither of us ever verbally acknowledged how weak he was becoming.

My life felt surreal. It was like I was living a life separate from my own. I maintained enough composure to capture a few pictures of our unique ceremony. Reverend D'Amico had us pose under the stained glass window representing the childless couple, which we found interesting since we had never shared that issue with him.

We later celebrated with family and friends before Bob, Brandie, and I drove up to our favorite place in the world, Yosemite National Park, to celebrate our second honeymoon. We invited my parents to come along, which they did, and it was a very emotional yet meaningful time together. Bob was struggling with pain but never, ever complained. And I carefully monitored his injections

Renewing Our Vows~June 21, 1981

every three hours. So many nights I stayed awake, worried I would sleep through a pain shot.

It was a sunny day in Yosemite, and I recall the warmth of the rocks beneath me as I sat in the sun in my black bikini, my body lean and bony.

"Wow, Snookie, I can't believe we are here," Bob said as he smiled at me. The clear blue sky and fresh mountain air permeated our senses, and the sound of the stream trickling below was relaxing and soothing. Bob wore his favorite Hawaiian shirt, which hid his frail frame. He had lost over seventy pounds, weighing in at around one hundred twenty—not a healthy weight for a man well over six feet tall. The two-year journey through colon cancer was wearing on both of us. But, the smiles on our faces reflected the hope and joy that still buoyed our spirits. We were not about to give up.

That evening we went to the old Wawona Hotel for a celebration dinner. Bob was experiencing so much pain that he and I walked out to our car for a much-needed pain shot and ultimately had to leave the restaurant early. Bob was unable to take it or fake it anymore. He felt bad since my folks had made the long drive up, but of course, they understood. And no doubt, they felt helpless under the circumstances.

We spent the last night in our cabin, but we all agreed to leave the next day. Not, however, before Bob did something that shocked me. Bob was an Eagle Scout as a young boy, and it was instilled in him to "leave the place better than you found it." I could not believe my eyes when I watched my thin, drawn husband chop a small pile of firewood to leave behind, possibly his final contribution to the family cabin in Yosemite. I later wondered if he somehow knew.

Eventually, we loaded our luggage in the car, and with our little Brandie in tow, we began the long drive back to San Diego. Mom and Dad left before us, so we were on our own now. I was the designated driver, while Bob reclined in his seat and rested.

He was pretty groggy between pain shots, so I relied on the radio and cassette player to keep me awake for the seven-hour journey while Bob mostly slept. For a lengthy stretch of road out of Yosemite, I drove in silence, absorbed in the myriad of thoughts swirling in my head. Periodically I glanced over at his tired, thin body and wondered how long he could continue like this. I softly took his hand and was thankful for its warmth and strength when he firmly grasped my palm. Deep in my spirit, I felt we were coming home for the last time, although I wrestled with myself not to give in to that thought. I so wanted to remain hopeful.

DEAR LOVER MY SMILE

WELL I STILL ANSWER YOU AND REALLY ALWAYS WILL. WE HAVE THE MOST TIME IN LOVE & CONSIDERATION FOR EACH OTHER AND WE JUST REALLY & MANY ARE THE BEST OF FRIENDS. YOU AND I GIVE OUR LIVES FOR EACH OTHER'S HAPPINESS WHICH IN TURN GENERATES HAPPINESS FOR EACH OF US AND US TOGETHER! I CAN'T REALLY GET THE MAGNITUDE ACROSS TO YOU OF HOW MUCH STRENGTH, LOVE & SUPPORT YOU HAVE GIVEN ME ALWAYS, BUT ESPECIALLY THROUGH THIS LAST BOUT OF HARDSHIP. I REALLY COULDN'T HAVE COME THROUGH & KEPT FIGHTING IF IT HADN'T BEEN FOR YOUR HELP, HONESTLY!! WE HAVE TO MAKE TIME FOR OURSELVES BECAUSE THERE IS JUST A MILLION PLACES WE WANT TO GO TO AND THINGS WE WANT TO DO AS A "WE". SO, THERE JUST SIMPLY HAS TO BE A LOT OF YEARS TOGETHER, LAUGHING, LOVING & BEING (US). I HAVEN'T REALLY HAD MUCH CHANCE TO GET YOU A PRESENT YET BUT WE MAYBE SHOULD CONSIDER A SUPER TRIP (TOGETHER, AS PRESENTS TO EACH OTHER JUST A THOUGHT, WE'LL SEE. TO US..... HEALTH, HAPPINESS AND ALL THE RIGHT DECISIONS, TOGETHER, FOREVER'. HAPPY 6TH OF MANY TO COME LOVER, AND MY DEEPEST DEEPEST THANKS TO YOU FOR TRULY THE HAPPIEST & BEST YEARS OF MY LIFE.

XXXXX
OOOOO
Love, Bob

JUNE 21ST, 1981
6TH YEAR OF THE BEST MARRIAGE I KNOW OF — OURS!!

I know I needn't tell you
That I love to have you near me.
Or what a comfort it has been
To have you there to cheer me--
I know I needn't tell you
You bring purpose to my life
Or that my joy has been complete
Since you became my wife--

I know I needn't tell you,
But I want to tell you still
That you mean everything to me
And you always will.

Happy Anniversary
With Love
I Love You
Bob

Bob's Last Card to Me~June 21, 1981

81

CHAPTER TEN

The Unexpected Decline Begins

AFTER RETURNING TO CARLSBAD, we spent several days recuperating from our long road trip. Being back in our home together was refreshing, like a giant soft pillow beckoning us to relax and enjoy. And it was nice to have a chance to unwind before the next follow-up with Bob's surgeon. It was time to see what was next in the treatment plan on the road to Bob feeling better.

Meanwhile, we made the regular morning trips to our local McDonald's to continue with what Bob called "Operation Stuff It".

"I gotta gain my weight back, Snookie Bear, and this is the best way to get the most bang for our buck!"

"You got it," I replied with a huge smile and a thumbs-up as we hopped in the car and headed to our nearest golden arches.

After consuming his usual Big Mac, large fries, and chocolate shake, we came home, and Bob needed to lie down, so he retreated to our bedroom. His legs and spine were in severe pain, and he had an irritating infection in his mouth. As the leg pain increased, it became more and more difficult for him to walk. One morning, when he awoke, he was unable to move. As his caregiver, I was weary, feeling frustrated and helpless that the injections did not keep the pain under control. So, once again, I contacted Bob's doctor. He was unavailable to take the call, but his nurse, Paige, increased the dosage of the pain injection, Dilaudid, the most intense pain medication I could provide him at home.

"Give him what he needs to keep the pain at bay," she told me. I felt frustrated but grateful for the call and short-term answer.

* * *

Sometimes my regrets haunt me. It was a lonely midweek afternoon when I gave Bob an injection, and he lay on the bed waiting for it to take effect. That could take as long as fifteen minutes while he writhed and moaned. Watching my precious husband in so much agony was devastating, and one particular afternoon, I could no longer take it. I needed to escape mentally, so I numbly wandered into the family room and turned on an *I Love Lucy* rerun. I needed comic relief. Suddenly, I heard Bob calling from the bedroom and immediately went to be by his side. He was teary-eyed when he asked where I had been.

"Please lie down with me, Snookie Bear. I need you."

"Oh baby, I am so sorry."

As I huddled near him, hot tears brimmed in my eyes, releasing some of my pent-up frustration and gut-wrenching fears. A foreboding dark cloud of terror loomed over me, reminding me that something awful would happen if things did not improve. I gently held him while the medicine eventually took hold, and his body finally relaxed. The injections were becoming more frequent, about every two hours. I struggled to keep a handle on when to give the next one before the previous one wore off. I constantly second-guessed myself and was, therefore, riddled with anxiety. I shuddered at the thought of a lapse, especially when excruciating breakthrough pain took over, yet I also feared the possibility of overmedicating him. I was overwhelmed but doing my darndest to manage the situation.

* * *

Finally, the day of our next appointment arrived, so Bob and I headed up to Los Angeles to meet with Dr. Sherman. I was anxious to confront him with some pointed questions about Bob's condition. When we checked in, the nurse drew his blood. Then we sat in the waiting room for quite some time before I walked over and asked the receptionist how much longer it would be. It was already forty-five minutes past our appointed time.

"Excuse me, but are we going to be seen sometime soon? My husband is uncomfortable sitting very long, and it has already been quite a while. He is in an awful lot of pain."

"Let me see what the hold-up is," she replied.

She eventually returned to the waiting area.

"I am so sorry, but an emergency came up, and Dr. Sherman had to leave. But he did ask me to tell you to give Bob whatever medicine he needed to feel comfortable." Bob and I looked at each other, completely speechless. It seemed so strange that with all we were experiencing, the doctor could not provide us even a couple of minutes to answer some questions. But we graciously thanked her and left, feeling dumbfounded and confused.

"Well, that was bogus," Bob said, rubbing his lower back with his fist as we got into the car. "Now what do we do?"

"I'll call him when we get home. This is unacceptable," I replied, trying to hide my anger and fear about the perplexing way the appointment had gone. It suddenly felt like we were isolated and abandoned.

I quickly discarded those feelings and turned my attention to Bob.

"Do you need a shot before we hit the road, sweetie? And we may as well stop for lunch if you feel up to it." Except for a quick drive-thru for a bite to eat, Bob slept most of the two-hour ride home, waking only to adjust the tennis balls he sat on, hoping for some relief from the excruciating pain in his hips. Alone in my head, which was never a good idea, I distracted myself as much as possible with music and the Friday traffic. But I could not stop thinking and wondering why our doctor chose not to see us. How could this be? I thought. How does a doctor not address an issue as serious as this? I felt helpless trying to make sense of it but knew it would not have been appropriate to complain or dispute what the nurse said. Doctors, in those days, were revered like God. So, I made a mental note to follow up on Monday morning. It was clear that the pain injections I was administering around the clock were not working

It was mid-July 1981 and a warm, sunny weekend when our cousins, Cindy and Jim, visited. A week had passed since we were together, and when they first saw Bob, it was noticeable that he had lost more weight. I knew this was partially due to his recent surgery, but being with him every day and night, I was not as aware until they subtly mentioned it. I then began to look at Bob through different eyes and realized I had refused to face reality. He had lost over eighty pounds from his regular weight, which I had also chosen to ignore. Instead, I continually tried to focus on our daily progress—and not give in to what was possibly happening.

After an enjoyable day and evening, we all went to bed. Bob, unusually sleepy all day, soon fell into a deep sleep. Around midnight, however, I woke up to him shaking violently, and when I touched his skin, he was burning hot. As I ran to grab the thermometer, I tossed a washcloth under the cold faucet. Meanwhile, he had managed to roll out of bed and was sitting upright on the floor in our bedroom. He appeared to be delirious, and when I took his temperature, it was 105 degrees. As I huddled over him and attempted to bring the fever down, I embraced him and reassured him that he would be all right.

And that is how my cousin Cindy found us when she instinctively woke up and came in to see if she could help.

"Is everything okay?" she said. "What can I do to help?" I will never forget how grateful I was that she was there and the peace I felt knowing we were not alone. I knew Bob did not want to go to the hospital, so with her help and support, we did our best to manage the situation at home.

The fever finally broke, and I made a mental note to ask what that was about when I called the doctor on Monday. We crawled back into bed, and Bob slept pretty well after that.

The next day, Sunday, Bob felt better when we woke up.

"Good morning! What should we do today?" I asked him when he finally wandered into the kitchen, where we were having coffee.

"How about we take a drive and show Cindy and Jim the property we bought with Ray."

We got ready and hopped into our car. After a pain injection, he walked us down the path of majestic eucalyptus trees that outlined the acreage. It amazed me that he managed to do this following the episode the night before, but his determination did not surprise me.

Afterward, we went to our all-time favorite deli for lunch. As we studied the menu, I noticed that something was different. The waitress went around the table to take our orders, and when she came to Bob, he was asleep. She diverted her eyes while I gently nudged him and pretended nothing was wrong. He immediately snapped back to reality and placed his order.

"Oh," he smiled, a bit confused. "I would like a corned beef on rye with french fries."

After that, he began to sleep more often, and I was positive I had overmedicated him. Cindy and Jim left that afternoon; I spent Sunday evening with Bob sleeping by my side. Admittedly, I was scared and overly anxious to contact our doctor the next day. The medication was not holding his pain, and I needed to find out what we could do to get the situation under control long-term. He could not do what he loved in life, including real estate, and I wanted to find out how we could help him return to normal.

The following morning, Monday, I put in a call to his doctor.

"He has a heavy surgery schedule today, but I will let him know you are eager to speak to him."

"Thank you, Paige," I responded. "I am worried about Bob and need to find out what we can do to help with his pain. The current plan is not working. We need to change his medication to something stronger so he can function better. He has things he wants to do." I also told her about the incident on Saturday night and how scary that was. She was sympathetic and told me she would have him call as soon as he had a break.

Bob slept most of the day while I tried to stay busy and not wander into my head. I called Cindy and told her I was waiting for a return call. I began to go into the what-ifs with her—what if there was not a better medicine to control his pain? What if it would always be like this? What if the cancer was back? While talking myself right into hysterics, her soothing, calming voice talked me 'off the ledge'.

"Try not to go too far ahead, Linda," she said. "There is no way to know how this will play out, and this is creating more anxiety for you. Try to stay in the now. Take some deep breaths to relax so you can be present for Bob."

Through my sobs, I agreed and thanked her. She was my rock.

"I cannot imagine what this must be like for you," she continued, "but please know that Jim and I are here for you always, so call us anytime."

Well, that worked—for a while.

I knew that Bob would give anything to live—to overcome this illness and enjoy a long, healthy life. But, deep down, I believed his spirit was conflicted. Was that even a possibility for him? I was unclear but desperately wanted to hang on to my hope, our hope, for as long as possible.

Later that afternoon, Ray came by and sat with me as I shared my concern about Bob being so sleepy lately and in extreme pain. I was confused and at a loss for what to do. I told him I had left a message for the doctor to discuss better pain management and his high fever on Saturday night.

"He cannot keep on like this, Ray. The doctor needs to change his meds. This is not working," I rambled on frantically.

I was grateful to have his company until he began to speak.

"Well, you know Bob is going to die, right?"

I glared at him in horror.

"That is not true, Ray—how can you say that? We are just having a setback and need to adjust his medications." I was appalled and angry that he would even suggest such a thing.

Suddenly the phone rang, and I ran into the other room to grab the call, hoping it did not wake Bob. It was Dr. Sherman. As soon as I heard his voice, I, in desperation, anxiously began to explain our dilemma.

"Dr. Sherman, Bob is still in horrible pain, and it's getting worse. I can no longer stand to watch him suffer like this—he will never get back to work in this condition. You need to prescribe a stronger medication...."

I could hear him inhale a deep breath as I continued to describe our situation, and with much sorrow in his voice, he interrupted me.

"Linda, the malignant cells have spread, and Bob is not going to get better. We have done all we could do." He paused for a brief second. "You are about to witness what it is like to die of cancer."

I closed my eyes and attempted to catch a breath while my hand tightly gripped the phone. My clammy palm barely held on while I tried to grasp what I had just heard. Or did I? Was this truly happening? Our doctor, who had been doing all he could over the past two years to save his life, was now betraying me, telling me my Bob was dying. In my wildest dreams, I did not expect this. My heart was hammering in my chest, and suddenly it felt like the room was spinning. I was stunned by what he was saying—his words were a knife piercing my soul, and the shock was more than I could bear. My Bob cannot die, not my Snookie Bear, not my prince. There must have been some mistake. The familiar knot of terror in my gut began to surface as I searched for words while fighting an oncoming panic attack.

"What are you saying?" I finally managed to whisper frantically into the phone. "I thought he was going to get better. How can you tell me this?"

Following a lingering pause, he tearfully responded. "The blood test last week showed the recurrence of cancer. I am so sorry, Linda." I could hear the sorrow in his voice.

All I managed to express was a moan as I struggled to speak; there were no words. I felt so defeated, so beaten up.

"What do I do now?" I barely uttered, hot tears burning down my cheeks.

"If it were me, and God forbid I should ever be in this position, I would do just what you are. Keep him at home as long as you can."

"I know that is what he would want, but can I do that?"

"Yes, as long as you can handle it and continue caring for him, that is the best situation. And Linda, please give him whatever pain medicine he needs to keep him comfortable. There is no limit now. It is just a matter of time. Again, I am so sorry. It is tragic to have this happen to such a lovely young couple as you two. We were all so hopeful."

As I cradled the receiver back onto the phone, I realized there was nothing more to say. I closed my eyes and tried hard to comprehend the words that burned deep in my inner being.

The words I had never wanted to hear hit me like an unexpected slap to my face, a punch in my gut. It was beyond belief. From the beginning, we thought we would beat it, that everything we had faithfully done guaranteed that Bob and I would live an ordinary life, the promised fairy tale. My young, naive mind never fathomed that Bob would not live. I had no idea or notion of that.

"Where are you, God?" I whispered. "How do I do this?"

Slowly, I dragged myself back to the family room, where Ray was waiting. Through tear-drenched eyes, I stared at him in a state of shock. Bob was asleep in our bedroom, or so we thought.

"Bob is going to die, Ray." In my quietest voice, I repeated what the doctor had said. He refrained from an "I told you so" just as Bob sauntered unsteadily into the room. I quickly ducked into the kitchen to wipe the tears from my face.

"Well, well, well….hello stranger!" Ray said as he stood up and gave him a gentle shoulder hug. I was praying he had not heard our conversation. Although Bob and I had promised not to keep secrets from one another, it felt like this was not the best time to share this new truth with him. He returned to bed before long, but his spirits were up during his visit with Ray. Bob could have coined the phrase "fake it til you make it."

Ray stayed with me for a while, but I had no words or emotions left. I was completely numb. He soon sensed I needed some time alone. I hugged him goodbye and went in to check on Bob. He was barely dozing and due for another pain injection. I kissed his cheek after the shot and gently tucked him in.

Alone in our family room, I poured a glass of wine and turned on some music. Snuggling into our comfy sofa, I knew I needed to digest this new information, but I had no idea where to begin. The thought of it all was terrifying as I attempted to process the conversation with our doctor and wrap my mind around what was ahead. I found myself utterly blindsided by that phone call, which, in turn, made me realize that I had been in denial. Hearing that Bob would eventually die from cancer hit me like a ton of bricks, but with good reason. No one had ever mentioned to us the possibility that Bob might not make it. The news we always received was hopeful and encouraging, and it was what we needed to keep going. My mind suddenly shifted to Bob and how I would ever tell him this truth. He was sleeping more often now but was so upbeat when awake. The last thing I wanted was to discourage him or take away any hope, yet there was that pledge of honesty between us. I had to trust that God would reveal the right timing. But, for now, every day we had together was precious, and my heart would not allow me to spoil any of what little time we had left.

Suddenly, out of nowhere, my thoughts became as dark as the night. I recalled conversations from a couple of weeks prior when Bob and I sat in a coffee shop having what was most likely our last lunch out together.

* * *

"There are a few things I want you to know." I slowly put down my fork and looked up, giving him my undivided attention.

Looking squarely into my eyes, with half a smile, he continued, "If and when I do die, I want you to keep my casket closed, especially if I'm having a bad hair day." That he would make light of it was no surprise, so I listened and nodded in agreement, assuring him that his wishes would be honored. I held back my emotions as much as possible, although he knew this was gut-wrenching.

"And I hope you can eventually sell the house, Linda, and find something more manageable. Our home would be a lot to keep up by yourself."

I sat in disbelief at this nightmare of a conversation. I nearly bit a hole in my lip as I attempted to hold back tears and promised him that if that ever did happen, I would sell the house when the time was right. As much as I wanted to scream—to cover my ears and tell him to STOP all this crazy talk—I knew I needed to be present as a strong wife and partner, aligned with him, and let him speak. And, for all I knew, he wanted to scream, too, but was handling it gingerly for my sake. It was unbearable to hear what he was telling me, but I had to respect him and listen. At that moment, it was not about me.

Bob reached across the table, took my hands in his, and as I sucked in my breath, he shared his final request.

"I want you to marry again, Linda. My only hope and prayer is that you can meet someone who loves you as much as I do." My widened eyes pierced his in sheer disbelief while our tears began to pool. That was the clincher, the final blow, the stab to my heart.

As the tears slowly streamed down my cheeks, I agreed that I would be open to that if the opportunity ever presented itself. I could not begin to think about it but hoped more than anything to give him peace of mind. It was the least I could do, after all. He was already enduring so much pain, both physically and emotionally. As heartbreaking as it was to hear his final wishes, it was a huge relief when he finished.

Now we can get back to our everyday life, I thought. It was nice that he had all those requests, but none of that would ever happen, I silently consoled myself. Denial had become my closest friend.

* * *

While I sat alone in our family room, reality slowly sank in. Did Bob already know? Did he have a sense from the beginning that he might not survive?

My face collapsed into my open, cupped palms as I tried to muffle the uncontrollable, heartbreaking sobs from deep within. I allowed myself to cry, my body heaving with each despairing breath. All the emotions I had held in for two long years and the insurmountable fear I would never permit myself to acknowledge were now bubbling to the surface. I was raw, broken, and scared to death. How could I watch my best friend die? How could this be happening? It wasn't the happily ever after that we had signed up for, nor what we had planned. How were we ever going to do this? Why us, God? Why Bob? I wrestled with those questions as night fell over our oasis in Carlsbad. Oh Bob, I cannot lose you, my Snookie Bear, I whispered into the darkness. Bob was peacefully asleep in the other room, and I knew I had to face this horrible truth and whatever else was ahead. I turned my tear-streaked face upward, begging God to help me, be with me, and carry me through.

It was late when I finally pulled it together and forced myself into bed. The large fan in our room merely swirled the warm July air around to make it bearable. I tossed all blankets aside and tried to get comfortable. Lying next to Bob was challenging. I wanted to put my hand on him, but a mere stroke or pat on his frail body would create pain and foster an agonizing moan. So, I fought the longing and gently took his palm in mine. As the moonlight shone through our bedroom window, I gazed at him long and hard and prayed I would always be aware when he needed a pain shot. And, worse yet, that I would not miss the moment of his passing.

While watching him breathe, his chest slowly rising and falling, I felt blessed to be lying next to this remarkable man. Suddenly, a tremendous wave of fear overcame me at the mere thought of my life without him. How could I do that? How would it happen, and when? I tried hard to squelch those fears and focus on the moment. I was determined not to miss anything; I was there for him no matter what, committed to remaining strong while I thought about how he had lived his life and made each day matter. It suddenly became clear that he knew his time on this earth was short.

Without warning, I recalled that conversation we had just before his initial diagnosis. We were getting ready for work together one morning, sharing hugs and kisses in our bathroom, as we often did. Bob suddenly gripped my shoulders, looked into my eyes, and said, "Try not to get too attached to me, Linda. I might not be around very long."

I was horrified that it might actually be a reality now. I had undoubtedly immediately pushed that thought from my mind until that moment when it came sneaking back to haunt me. Once again, tears spilled from my eyes as I silently cried myself to sleep.

The next day, after a restless night, I instinctively knew that if that were true, I needed to contact family and close friends to allow them to come to see him and say their goodbyes. I tried to time my phone calls when he was asleep, but I will never know if he overheard me.

Later that afternoon, the doorbell rang, and surprisingly, Bob was up and about and went to the door. It was a good friend of his, Kevin, from his real estate office.

"Hey, Buddy! It has been a while. How are you doing?" while exchanging a friendly hug.

"Oh, I'm hanging in there, Kevin," Bob said. "How are things at the office?"

"It's moving along, Bob, but the market sure is slowing down. Hope you will be back soon. I just wanted to say hi."

"Thanks for coming by, Kev—so nice of you. Hey, say hi to everyone for me."

I can only imagine how hard that was for both of them; Bob tried his best to hide the truth, including the pain he felt from a simple hug, and Kevin surely noticed his decline.

Slowly, throughout the week, family and friends arrived to spend time with Bob, some for a brief visit, others to stay for a while. Soon our house was filled with loved ones who brought meals and lots of love. Since Bob was now mostly bedridden, we all took turns sitting at his bedside. Brandie happily snuggled under the covers of our king-size bed, staying close to him. She rarely left his side, in bed, on the sofa in the family room, or lying outside on a lounge chair by the pool.

On Saturday, July 25th, my friend Cheryl, who I had known since first grade, visited us with her husband, Brian. She was an RN at Cedars-Sinai and proved to be my primary source of support during our times there.

During her visit, she helped me change Bob's colostomy bag while she assessed the situation. She was honest and direct when she told me I needed help. Before she and Brian left, she handed me a piece of paper with a phone number.

"You need to call hospice," she gently told me.

"What is hospice?" I asked her, never having heard of it.

"They will come to help you," she replied. "You should call them Monday morning."

"I am not interested in having a stranger help me, Cheryl. I promised Bob I would be there for him forever, until death do us part, and I meant it." Hot tears burned in my tired eyes.

She nodded in understanding but was concerned as she encircled me into her arms. I slipped the paper into my pocket and reluctantly assured her I would call, though no part of me wanted someone else caring for Bob. At the same time, however, I was unfamiliar with caregiver burnout or how long one could continue to do it alone. I silently decided to find out on my own.

Later that day, family and friends staying with us conferred and agreed to gather in our bedroom that night. It was unclear how it all occurred, but a predestined, appointed group of over twenty loved ones came together around Bob. Present in the group were his childhood best friends since age 8, Rocky and John, and his brother Chris, who shared stories from the past and present. I could not have orchestrated it myself, even if I had tried. It was a warm, balmy evening, and the windows were wide open with the hope of an ocean breeze for some relief. Our large fan swirled the warm air left over from the hot day while popular tunes from Air Supply, Jim Croce, Foreigner, and John Lennon played softly in the background.

Our time together was reminiscent, tearful, and ever so meaningful. "Remember when we did this and that? We had avocado fights, blew up mailboxes with M-80s, played tricks on neighbors, took journeys on our bikes, and stayed under the radar with our crazy schemes to cause just enough uproar but not (always) get into trouble?"

I knew that even though Bob was somewhat out of it, mainly due to his pain medication, he knew who was there, what was said, and quite possibly reflected on those memories himself. And because it was such an encouraging, energizing time for him, I did not have the heart to tell him his friends had come together to say goodbye.

As his dear friend, John, recently recalled, "Bob was our leader. He was charismatic, a guy-type-of-guy, an Eagle Scout, raised with high values, integrity, morals, and faith. He never discriminated against his friends regarding color, race, or nationality. Whoever he made friends with—well, they were his friends."

He went on to remember, "Bob loved that celebration, Linda. What a gift you provided that allowed him to focus on something other than the pain and possible fear he was feeling. While he sat up in bed, he listened carefully, grinned, laughed, and grimaced in pain. And I truly believe it helped him when the time came to move on. I will never forget that night—a wonderful event, a bittersweet time of pain and love."

It was easy to see that Bob's life held meaning for the countless lives he had touched in his short time here, evident not only by how many came to celebrate him but the stories that went on and on into the wee hours of the night. Who can say that at twenty-six years old? It was a remarkable tribute to and celebration of an amazing young man—while he was still here. We concluded our evening with a "Bob quote," which he often used to navigate his cancer journey.

Whenever anyone would ask him how he was, he would smile broadly and say, "I am doing the best I can with what I have to work with." Never a complaint, but instead a positive attitude every time. How he did it, I have no idea.

After everyone had left the room and we were alone in our bed, Bob gazed at the corner of our bedroom. "Look at all the colors," he said softly. For a brief, lucid moment, his eyes focused intently on one particular spot.

With surprise in his voice, he smiled and said, "Hi Dad!" To this day, I do not believe that this incident was a result of medication, hallucination, or lack of oxygen. I'm certain he was clearly seeing where he was soon heading, and was not only excited, but filled with peace and joy.

The next day, Sunday, the 26th, Bob was more alert than usual and responded to everyone who came to see him. When my dad went to sit with him, he was receptive and, to our surprise, sat up on the side of the bed to eat some applesauce, which my dad gladly fed him. When I walked into the room and saw his lean legs dangling over the edge of the bed, I gasped and realized it had been several days since I had seen him upright. For a split second, I felt encouraged.

It was all a dream, I secretly whispered to myself. I knew it was not real. Bob is going to make it after all.

Sleep-deprived, with one foot in the land of denial, I allowed myself a little hope. But shortly after his sudden burst of energy, he returned to bed and fell fast asleep. I was instantly snapped back into reality, returned to my wits, and became aware that I now needed to be true to myself and accept what was happening. I could no longer let my fantasy mind get the better of me.

Bob was well under 120 pounds by then and, as if having cancer was not enough, thrush—an infection that included blisters and much discomfort—had invaded his throat. Additionally, he had severe bone pain where the tumor was growing and spreading. Imagining what that man was going through at such a young, undeserving age made me shudder. He was dying to live, but instead he was dying. Oh, how my heart ached as I watched him struggle through this, most of the time feeling helpless in my ability to control the relentless agony.

It was later that afternoon when I requested some time alone with Bob. I had an insight, a prompting I could not ignore, as I went into our room to spend a private moment with my prince, the love of my life. I suddenly wanted as much time as I could get with him, and I didn't want to share or miss a minute. Family and friends were in other parts of the house while I lay beside him on our bed. I suddenly realized that moment might be our last intimate time together.

Bob and I had music playing constantly. As we lay there together, Diana Ross and Lionel Richie sang "Endless Love" on our stereo, followed by Journey with "Open Arms." Our standup fan continued to do its best to chill the hot summer air; it could not have been a more perfect and loving scenario for what was about to transpire.

Wavering in and out of consciousness and talking very little by then, Bob was still communicating with me through his eyes. He trusted me to the fullest, and his eyes deeply pierced mine. It was as if we could see beyond and peer through the window of our souls. I have never felt as connected to another human being as I did to Bob—mind, body, and spirit. And he had often told me the only way he could feel any closer to me would be if he were under my skin.

That soulful connection was all we had left now, and I had to depend on that to express to him the heart-wrenching truth I had been holding inside. Instinctively, I knew that Bob was going to die soon. It was time to share what Dr. Sherman had told me. During our short life together, Bob and I never had any secrets from one other, so why change now?

But all I wanted to do right then was enjoy every second we had left and physically experience the deep love we felt for one another in this final time together. I was blessed to have this gift of time with him that would never happen again.

I snuggled as close as possible without hurting his broken body. I then gently moistened and kissed his dry, cracked lips. With my prompting, we curled our bodies together, and as frail and exhausted as Bob was, he seemed to have just enough energy to express his deep love for me as we began to shower one another with soft, tender kisses. I wanted to lie in his arms forever and stay connected to that sweet moment.

After a long, tender kiss, I told him, "I could never love you more if I tried, Snookie Bear and, because I do, I need to share something from the deepest part of my soul."

"You are the most amazing husband and best friend I ever dreamed of having, and I am so grateful for that day you said hello to me after our health class. Our lives together have been magical since then; to live my life without you is unimaginable."

Gazing deep into his eyes, I whispered softly, "Dr. Sherman finally called us this week." His eyes widened as he struggled to sit up. I tenderly pressed my palm to his chest to calm him and inhaled a deep breath while I continued. "The blood test was not good. Cancer has returned, Snookie Bear."

His look of surprise confirmed my gut feeling that he was striving to fight for his life and mine. He, too, had been in denial. Our mutual desire to conquer this cancer was evident at this point. We were so young, so naive, and so determined for him to live! How could anyone or anything rob us of this?

Suddenly, a nudge in my spirit prompted me to say something, possibly the bravest thing I had ever done.

His eyes lovingly locked with mine in total trust, and while my hands cradled his face, I softly proceeded.

"I want you to stop fighting this for me, Bob. I promise I will be okay. When it feels right for you, and when God beckons you, I want you to take his hand."

As I spoke those words, he stared deep into my eyes, and I could tell he understood. Tears dropped down my cheeks while I carefully held him in my arms, gently kissed him, and felt his heart beat very slowly, his breathing labored. He was dozing in and out of consciousness, but the look on his face was relaxed and showed sheer peace as my soft tears began to fall, streaking his pale face.

As hard as that was for me, it was more painful to watch him suffer any longer, continue the injections, and see yet another bone protrude from his yellowing, frail body. That was more than I could bear, especially now that I knew the truth. I was amazed I could say those words to him, but I knew my inner voice was not one I could ignore.

After a while, I needed to let others spend this precious time with him, so I pulled myself together, helped Bob back into his scrubs, and called out for my cousin Jim to come and sit with him while I took a moment to collect myself.

Surprisingly, I felt an overwhelming peace in my spirit as the reality of the situation slowly began to sink in. Our hopes and dreams of a long life together were slipping away, and I felt myself surrendering. I briefly shared with Jim what I had told Bob so he would know and be aware before he went to his bedside.

"We had some sweet time alone," I said, "and I let him know he is not going to get better." I glanced sadly at Jim and whispered, "I told him to go with God."

He hugged me while I wept, and then he hurried back into our bedroom while I went to our family room to let the others know what was coming.

We continued taking turns sitting by his bedside, holding his hand while watching his chest slowly rise and fall. By now, he was peaceful and not at all responsive. And just a few hours later, shortly after midnight, Jim nodded to me as I held on to Bob while he took three shallow breaths, followed by a distinct rattle, which left him completely silent and still.

At 12:17 a.m., I watched the love of my life transcend from this life into the next as he took the hand of God. Still lying in my arms, I continued to kiss and hold him tight. At that moment, I visibly saw all of the promises of heaven come to light as I witnessed his spirit leave his earthly body and transcend into the next realm.

"I will see you later, my love," I cried out to him. I could not utter the word goodbye.

While Air Supply softly sang, "The One That You Love," I curled up beside him. Clinging fiercely to his now cool and slightly stiff body, I tried to grasp what had just happened. Even though I had known in my head that he was going to die, the profound absence of his earthly presence was shocking. As he lay there, quiet and motionless, with a serene look on his face, I was adamant that I did not want him to leave. I wanted to cherish that moment for as long as I could. And my mind kept playing tricks on itself, trying to convince me that this was all a bad dream. I just knew, at any moment, he would sit up and tell me it was all a joke. It would have been just like him to do that.

I suddenly realized that Brandie had disappeared sometime during the evening. The three of us needed to be together, I thought. Not wanting to leave his side, I called to her from the bedroom, and she came running in, sprang up on the bed, and, after assessing the situation, she quickly jumped off and ran away. It was unlike her not to be near us, but she sensed something was wrong. It was an eerie time, and as I tried to imagine where Bob was now, I lay close and held tightly to his lifeless body.

That poor body had been through so much yet fought to the bitter end for dear life. I glanced up in the corner of our bedroom and imagined his spirit looking down on the scene below. I tried so hard to hold on to that moment, so much so that when the paramedics and police arrived, whom Jim had dutifully called, I gripped Bob even harder and refused to let them take him.

Endless tears streamed down my face while overwhelming panic welled up inside me.

"Please," I begged, "just let him stay with me one more night."

They assured me they were only there as a formality, since Bob died at home, without hospice.

"How old was your father?" one of the officers asked me.

Glaring at him, I grabbed hold of Bob and defensively replied, "Bob is my husband, not my father." I guess I had ignored how much his body had aged due to emaciation. "Over there," I cried, pointing to a healthy picture of Bob on our dresser. "That is how he normally looks."

Soon the coroner arrived, followed by the mortuary van. Hysteria had overcome me as his friend John gently peeled me away from Bob and guided me out of the room. Later I realized they were all trying to protect me from the next ordeal.

But, when I heard strange voices coming from our bedroom, I bolted back in there just in time to watch them hoist his limp body onto a black vinyl-covered gurney. As the mortician slowly wheeled him out of our double front doors, I desperately cried out, "No! No! Take me with him," while I sobbed hysterically. Meanwhile, Rocky softly slipped a little pillow under his head.

Clutching my chest, I stood with my friends on our porch and wailed as they rolled Bob down the sidewalk and into the back of the nearby van. Jim, Rocky, and John walked solemnly alongside the gurney. Ray, who had gone home a couple of hours prior, walked up the sidewalk just as they lifted Bob into the van. He came directly to me and held me in his arms while I sobbed. Gingerly, he guided me to our family room, where someone handed me a glass of wine. I fell to the floor in a heap of horror, panic, and dread, unable to grasp what was happening. I was completely numb.

"Endless Love" was playing on the radio. I closed my eyes and listened while, in my head, our final conversation replayed. Had I willed him to die? I asked myself. I knew I was not to blame, but would he still be here had I not had that final talk with him? Guilt and fear were consuming me.

I shared this dilemma with our friends and family, who assured me I did the right thing.

"You gave Bob permission and the peace he needed to pass," John said. "If you had held back on that freedom, the inevitable, along with the agony, would have been prolonged. Linda, what you did for Bob was a gift."

Little did I know I would continue to give this gift many times in the days ahead. Bob had graciously taught me how to let go, which, in turn, later allowed me to help others in the same situation.

After a few more hours of reliving what Bob had experienced and trying to grasp what had finally happened, I was eventually getting sleepy but knew what I now had to face. I needed to go back into our bed and sleep alone, as hard as that would be. Meanwhile, my mom had changed the sheets, so our bed was fresh and ready. Initially, I resented that she did that, as I longed to lie where Bob had been, feel his presence, and breathe in his final scent. But, brushing those thoughts aside, I silently told myself I needed to go back in there that night, or I probably never would. I knew I had to be brave and take that next big, painful step forward. It was the beginning of many challenges yet to come.

As the night sky slowly began to break into daylight, I wandered toward our bedroom So, with Brandie by my side, I slowly crawled in and curled up on Bob's side of the bed. Thankfully, I soon fell deep into sleep. Thus, I felt a glimmer of hope that I might survive beyond this incomprehensible and devastating night.

CHAPTER ELEVEN

The Morning After Bob Went to Heaven

I awoke in a state of true disbelief
But oddly I felt a sense of relief.
I reached over yet knew you were not there
Your absence in our bed was more than I could bear.
I longed so to see, feel, and hold onto my man
But knew deep in my soul God had another plan.

IT WAS THE MORNING of July 27, 1981, and considering how late I finally fell asleep, I woke up early in a confused daze. At first, I had to collect myself and my thoughts to determine what might have been a dream and what had actually occurred.

As I began to stir, my first instinct was to reach over to the other side of our bed and gently touch Bob. When I realized he wasn't there, a numbness came over me, and a jolt of fear spilled through my body. I felt empty of emotion and perhaps a bit dead inside myself.

When I slowly opened my eyes and glanced across the room, I saw

Bob's glasses and the watch I had given him the previous Christmas lying neatly atop our dresser. I lay there frozen for a moment as the reality of the night before suddenly hit me. For some unknown reason, however, I felt considerably calm. I knew that Bob was gone, and I was alone on his side of our bed.

Slowly, I allowed the memories of the all-too-new events from the night before to sink in. Although the sheets on the bed were fresh and clean, the harsh fact remained; I was lying in our bed by myself.

Glancing around our room, our sanctuary for the past two years, I could easily visualize Bob sitting in the comfy chair in the corner, standing at his closet door, or lying beside me in our bed.

My thoughts were muddled, and I could not fathom how I ended up in our bed alone. With my face buried deep in Bob's pillow, I began to sob uncontrollably. I had no idea how I would ever face life without him.

Suddenly, I spontaneously decided to pick up the phone and randomly call someone to tell them of the news. As I look back on that time, I know I was not in my right mind but was desperately seeking to make the nightmare seem somewhat normal, to any degree I could.

So, without hesitation, I called my friend Sharon with whom I used to work at the job I initially found when Bob and I moved to San Diego. I had honored Bob's request that I keep his illness confidential, so although I worked directly next to Sharon during our cancer journey, I could not tell her why some days I arrived at work teary-eyed or frequently called Bob to check on him. I knew she must have wondered what I was hiding. As I dialed her extension, I held my breath and soon heard her voice.

"Hi Sharon, it's Linda. Can you talk?"

"Of course," she answered cheerfully. "It's been a while, my friend. How are you doing?"

"I know it has, Sharon, and my time away has not been easy. I have some bad news to share with you, which will probably come as a shock." As I lay in our bed, my head on his pillow, I drew a deep breath and said, "Bob has been fighting cancer, Sharon. I quit work to stay home and care for him." I paused.

"He died last night."

I suddenly heard myself saying it aloud, and my body trembled with angst. There it was, the truth I had never wanted to face. The deep, dark secret that Bob and I shared and that I held inside for two long years was finally seeping out of me. My body ached with emotion and pain. At first, it felt like I was betraying Bob, but I slowly allowed myself to give in to the reality that he was no longer with me. I did not need to keep our secret any longer...that secret we both so valiantly shared.

There was a long silence, finally broken by a gasping sob. It was clear Sharon was stunned by my words.

"I knew something was wrong, Linda, but I never wanted to pry. I trusted you would share with me when you felt like you could." I heard her softly sniffling. We chatted a little longer, and I explained some of the details. But the conversation was a blur to me. I told her to feel free to share the update with others in our office, as I knew I would need their support in days to come. Clearly in shock, I prayed that the emotional numbness I felt that morning would continue to envelop me.

Somehow, I managed to crawl out of bed and found myself in the bathroom in a total daze. I brushed my teeth in a complete stupor and wandered out to the kitchen, where others were already having coffee. Several of our friends were in the front yard, mowing the lawn, gardening, and tending to the things Bob and I had recently neglected. Others were cleaning the pool and the house and preparing food.

Mindlessly, I poured myself a cup of coffee, fell into a chair at our kitchen table, and stared blankly out the window to the ocean. Bob and I loved our view. It was one of the many reasons we chose that home. Now, it was painful to even look out at what only days before we had enjoyed together. I can't even describe what I was feeling in the moment. I knew I was still alive, and Bob was not. In the blink of an eye, he was gone. And I was left to carry on without him.

Suddenly the phone rang, and slowly, numbly, I forced myself to answer.

"Hello," I said in a dull tone. It was our dentist's office.

"Hi! Just calling to remind Bob of the appointment for his cleaning this afternoon," she said in an overly chipper voice.

Quite politely, I told her he was unable to make it.

"Bob died last night," I heard myself say for the second time that morning. Later I thought that might have been a bit harsh, but what else could I have said? It was the truth. Bob no longer needed to have his teeth cleaned. How did that possibly matter now? It was just another brutal reminder. As I hung up the phone, tears came streaming down my cheeks.

My mom, keeping a keen eye on me from the kitchen, came over and folded me into her arms. Although it was comforting at the moment, I knew nothing could console me or make it all better, much less take it away. I felt that familiar knot in my tummy grow tighter as I reluctantly allowed myself to weep on her shoulder, slowly surrendering my stoicism. My body heaved deep, desperate sobs as I wailed. Why did this have to happen? My poor mom was crying with me, and as I look back now, I can't imagine what that must have been like for her. Her pain was two-fold; she was grieving for her daughter, and also for the loss of her son-in-law. What a helpless feeling that must have been.

Aimlessly, I went about the day, so thankful for all those staying with me in our home. We were all grieving together, as everyone was deeply affected by Bob's life and how he died. Bob had excellent relationship skills and treated those fortunate to know him with care and concern. He was a man of his word and took time to know people, foster relationships, and be a true friend. He had the gift of making people feel comfortable and accepted for who they were, which is why, forty years later, his name still comes up often.

The rest of the week was a blur. More friends arrived from out of town; there were so many guests, and all stayed at our house. I was grateful to be surrounded by so much love and support. Everyone brought food, and Mom kept the huge coffee urn brewing day and night. My dad was there also; he took the week off to be with me. Both he and my mom were concerned about my psychological well-being, and rightfully so. Undeniably, I was not myself.

After contacting Reverend D'Amico on Tuesday and asking him to preside at the memorial service, I had to select the outfit Bob should wear in his casket. If you have never done this, you can probably imagine it is a rather peculiar task. How does one, first of all, even picture their twenty-six-year-old husband in a casket, let alone decide what he should wear for the occasion?

"You've got to be kidding," I told my friends and family. "Bob would surely be laughing right now and most likely opt for his green surgical scrubs if he were here." And, trust me, that was an option on the list. But, Bob also loved wearing Hawaiian print shirts, and I had recently made him a couple of new ones when he lost so much weight. I considered that idea but finally decided on the suit he wore when we renewed our wedding vows. That was a happy day for him, and I longed to picture him as my forever groom. It just seemed right and somehow appropriate.

So, along with a couple of friends, I went to the mortuary to deliver his clothes. It felt eerie to fathom that Bob was somewhere in the building when we walked in. After handing the bag of clothing to the funeral director, I sat down to discuss the final details of the viewing on Thursday evening and the funeral the following day.

Suddenly, I flashed again to the conversation Bob and I had over lunch one day, shortly before his decline, instructing me to keep the casket closed if his hair did not look good. I remembered being so upset that he was even talking that way, but now, as reality hit again, I knew I needed to honor his wishes. I requested that the viewing be private, exclusively for family and a group of invited friends. And during the funeral, I asked that the casket be closed. I did not want anyone who had not seen Bob at the end of his life to view him in his current condition. He would never forgive me!

Somehow I had the insight and courage to make those and other decisions, but it didn't feel like it was me. Emotionally, I was not even present. So, again, God and Bob were guiding me along. And I know Bob was smiling down on me for keeping the lid closed.

"Good job, Snookie Bear," I could hear him say.

I was not sure whether to smile or once again burst into tears. Thankfully, the numbness prevailed and allowed me to persevere through the remainder of the week, one day at a time.

The next morning, Wednesday, out of the blue, I told Esther, "I need to get my hair done."

I suppose that was a common thing to do when life is in turmoil. She was surprised at my request, but we made an appointment for the following day and went to my favorite salon. I was trying to do something tangible to feel alive, and in retrospect, I can see that it did help me move forward.

A piece of me felt dead inside, but instinctively I knew I needed to nurture the little bit of life I had left to prevent falling into a pit of depression. It was unclear how I knew this, but undeniably, God had His hand on me. And there was no doubt Bob did, as well.

My poor hairdresser was horrified and speechless when I told her my husband had died just days before I was getting my hair cut. I'm sure I had never mentioned his illness to her previously. I was numb.

Now, a few words about viewings. I had been to those of others, including my in-laws, and I knew that it was a proper, traditional thing to do. But, as I thought about it realistically, I did not get it. Not to sound sarcastic or disrespectful, but gathering to look at a lifeless person in a wooden box, suitably posed by some stranger, is creepy.

But, inevitably, Thursday evening arrived, and I knew I had to muster up all my courage while I rode with Rocky and Esther to the viewing. With butterflies fluttering in my tummy, I entered the mortuary and followed the others into the room. The anticipation of how Bob would look made me anxious, as I had not seen him since he was wheeled from our bedroom only three days prior.

"Lord, please give me strength," I whispered while forcing myself to walk up to the casket. Rocky and Jim had locked arms with me, and I gasped when I saw my young husband peacefully lying there, his hands carefully folded across his chest.

Instantly, I leaned down to kiss his cold, taut lips and nestled my head near his heart, while gently taking his stiff, unfeeling palm into mine. I placed a final card in his hands, one I had written to go with him forever. I was sure it was difficult for everyone there to watch, but I also knew this was the last time I would see and touch his earthly body, and I wanted to make it last as long as possible. Though fear loomed in my tummy, I felt God's hand on my shoulder as I tenderly placed my hand on Bob's heart.

The sight of his beautiful face would be etched forever in my memory, and his spirit deeply immersed in my heart and soul. There were several of us in that little room glancing at Bob. Since we had all been through his final battle together, no one was shocked by the appearance of his exhausted, frail body. Instead, we all saw strength and peace while he finally rested pain-free after his unrelenting struggle.

I had brought Bob's glasses with me, as I had watched my Aunt Juanita put Uncle Dick's glasses on him in his casket a few months earlier. I debated whether to put them on him during the wake, as it seemed somewhat ridiculous since his eyes were closed, and he appeared asleep. But in retrospect, he did look more like Bob, were that even possible. His calm, lifeless body that had been through so much appeared peaceful despite the wear and tear.

When it was time to leave, I gently removed his glasses to take them home with me and gave him one last, lingering kiss, praying he was at peace and that I would one day see him again.

We left the mortuary quietly that night, solemn and grief-stricken. There was nothing positive about this experience except that Bob was no longer in pain.

On the ride back home, I asked Rocky to stop at a gas station, where I called the mortuary from a payphone to confirm that they would not let anyone else in to view Bob. It was over now, and those who came to see him with me had come and gone. I knew the local newspaper had published his obituary, but no one else needed to see him. The coffin would close, and that would be it. He did not want people looking at him—especially if his hair looked funky. He made me promise.

I was thankful when I returned

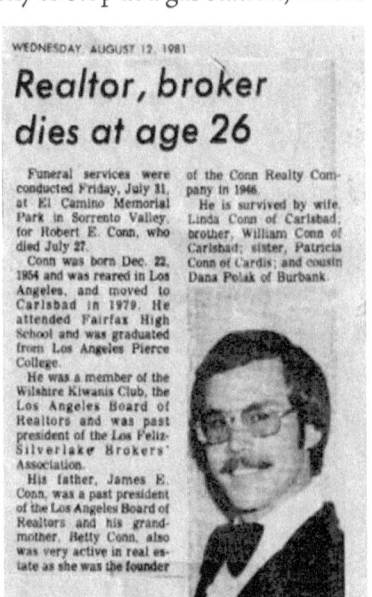

WEDNESDAY, AUGUST 12, 1981

Realtor, broker dies at age 26

Funeral services were conducted Friday, July 31, at El Camino Memorial Park in Sorrento Valley, for Robert E. Conn, who died July 27.

Conn was born Dec. 22, 1954 and was reared in Los Angeles, and moved to Carlsbad in 1979. He attended Fairfax High School and was graduated from Los Angeles Pierce College.

He was a member of the Wilshire Kiwanis Club, the Los Angeles Board of Realtors and was past president of the Los Feliz-Silverlake Brokers' Association.

His father, James E. Conn, was a past president of the Los Angeles Board of Realtors and his grandmother, Betty Conn, also was very active in real estate as she was the founder of the Conn Realty Company in 1946.

He is survived by wife, Linda Conn of Carlsbad; brother, William Conn of Carlsbad; sister, Patricia Conn of Cardis; and cousin Dana Polak of Burbank.

113

home with those lifelong friends at my side. I was not alone and I knew Bob had his hand in that. Our family and friends made an excruciatingly painful situation bearable.

The following day, I woke up early and attempted to prepare myself mentally for what was ahead. The funeral was at one that afternoon, and the mortuary had arranged for a limo to pick me up at eleven. I had a select few to ride in it with me, including my sister, brother/sister-in-law, and others in my family. I knew I would need all the support I could get.

It seemed to take me forever to get ready, probably because I had to keep reapplying make-up since the flow of tears was so unpredictable. And how does one even prepare for the memorial service of their soulmate, after all? There did not seem to be a guidebook available on that subject.

When I finally put on the dress I had worn for our wedding vow renewal the month before, I heard my father outside my bedroom door.

"They will be there any minute, sweetie. Are you almost ready?"

Predictably, he worried I might be late and hold things up, being the dad that he was. My goal, however, was to be ready as much as possible, both physically and emotionally, so I started becoming irritated with him.

"Do you really think they will start without me, Dad?" my eyes again welled up with fresh tears.

He walked away and never said another word to hurry me along. And I made a mental note to keep my anger in check as I realized it was one of many emotions bubbling barely below the surface.

When the limo arrived, we all got in, and as it drove us slowly out of the neighborhood, I realized I had forgotten something. Bob had written a message for his friend John when John's dad passed away a few years prior, and I wanted to have it read at the graveside service.

"Excuse me, I forgot something," I called to the limo driver. "Could you please turn around? It will only take me a minute."

I did not even look at my father to avoid his look of disdain. I did not care. The day belonged to Bob, and I was determined to make it the best I could. And that message was a significant part.

Ultimately, we arrived at the mortuary with plenty of time, and I immediately saw and greeted Reverend D'Amico, who had driven down from Los Angeles to perform the service. We exchanged a meaningful hug as tears pooled in my eyes. He had come full circle with Bob; he baptized him as a young boy, married the two of us twice, and now was going to bury him. I knew this day was sad for him, also, as he was fond of Bob and his family. It must have been infrequent that he blessed a complete life like this.

When I peered out from the side room reserved for family, I watched as the chapel filled up quickly. At my request, there were large, life-size photos of Bob surrounding his beautiful closed casket, along with the spray of red roses I had chosen for him, draped across, topped with BOB, I LOVE YOU in gold foil letters.

The casket had been selected earlier that week by my cousins, Cindy and Jim, who thankfully took it upon themselves to make the final arrangements. Jim referred to it as the 'Cadillac of Coffins'. He wanted Bob to go out in style, and since they knew that would have been a difficult decision for me, they spared me. I am forever grateful to them. Jim, John, Rocky, Bill, Ray, and my dad solemnly carried Bob in his closed casket into the mortuary so the service could begin.

Reverend D'Amico gave us a beautiful word picture of his life, from a young boy to now, and shared the happy times he spent with Bob and his entire family. He threaded it with scripture, hope, love, and respect.

Next, my cousin, Jim, delivered the eulogy for Bob:

* * *

TRIBUTE TO ROBERT EMMETT CONN
December 22, 1954 - July 27, 1981

"I would like to begin by saying Bob was the speechmaker and as most of you know, public speaking was one of Bob's fortés. But with his help, maybe I can get through this.

Bob was born in Los Angeles shortly before Christmas in 1954 - 26 years ago. He was the oldest of three children, having a sister, Patty, and a brother, Bill, both of whom loved and admired him a great deal. He attended Fairfax High School, obtained his degree at Pierce College, where he met his beautiful wife, Linda, and attended real estate classes at Los Angeles Valley College and Mount San Antonio.

Bob was a doer. He accomplished more in 26 years than some people ever achieve. He was an Eagle Scout, received many awards for marksmanship in the ROTC at Pierce College, was a member of the Pierce College swim team and a member of the Los Angeles Board of Realtors. As I said, Bob was a doer. He was also the youngest member of the Kiwanis Club and the youngest President of the Los Feliz/Silverlake Real Estate Brokers Association in 1979. Bob was especially proud of this because his dad was also President of that organization around 1960.

Bob was a man of tremendous strength and courage. As most of you know, his father died when Bob was still a boy in college, leaving behind Conn Realty.

Bob entered real estate school, obtained his license, and took his dad's place at Conn Realty. He demonstrated his courage again when he decided to leave Conn Realty and moved to Carls-

bad.

But his greatest challenge came two years ago when he found out he had colon cancer. But Bob found humor even in this situation. He often laughed about how his mind was a roadmap of all the porta-potties at all the construction sites in San Diego County.

Bob never lost his sense of humor. For example, during the times he was in the hospital, Linda always stayed with him and, of course, he always wore his surgeon's outfit with his name on it. One night a new nurse came into his room and was sure she had found a doctor sleeping with a patient. Bob thought that was pretty funny, but Linda was really embarrassed.

Another time while Bob was waiting for the x-ray technician to come, he pulled the sheet over his head just to shake the technician up.

And my favorite story is about the time the nurse kept asking Bob for a urine sample. So he gave her one. The next time she came in he had filled up another specimen bottle with apple juice. Bob asked her if she still needed a urine sample. When she said, "No," he unscrewed the lid and drank it. The nurse thought he had gone nuts. Bob always kept the nurses on their toes and Linda's spirits up.

Bob had a sensitive and considerate side, too. He loved Linda, his family, and friends. After he was taken to each of his surgeries, red roses were always delivered to Linda in the waiting room with a loving note from Bob. During his second surgery, he even had flowers for Linda's mother because it happened to be her birthday.

Bob didn't believe that death meant we have to say

"good-bye." He always felt his father's presence around him; and don't be surprised if you often feel Bob's presence around you. If you have a problem, ask Bob —- I'm sure he'll help you. He would want everyone here to remember the fun times, the serious moments and the good memories he left us — but most of all to remember him as a man of strength, courage and full of love.

Bob was a special person to all of us, so here is a special way to share with you some of Bob's favorite pastimes; and after the graveside gathering let's join each other at Linda's house to honor Bob.

Thanks for helping me through this, Bob."

* * *

Next, family and friends had put together a slide show featuring happy photos of Bob throughout his life. The slide show played while "Time in a Bottle," by Jim Croce, and "My Way," by Frank Sinatra, echoed throughout the chapel.

We then gathered at the graveside for the final blessing, and I had someone read the message Bob had written for John and his family when they lost their father. It felt only natural to share something at his service that he had personally written to comfort someone else:

> "As a seed drops and a tree grows, so life grows. As the tree grows and expands, the roots go deep. As the main branch, the leader, dies and falls to the ground, a life passes. But as the lead branch falls and covers the roots, helping them grow, the living tree continues to grow, following the path of the lead branch. The tree grows on even better. You must all work together and force your tree to live."
>
> ~ Robert Conn, at age 21

It was touching to hear those words spoken that he had written to console others; it was as though he were there, talking to all of us. Bob was a leader for many and, in a short time, made an impression on others through how he lived—even to his last day.

We laid Bob to rest under a shady tree in The Garden of Love section of the cemetery, where I will eventually join him. Although sadness consumed me, I felt peaceful and hopeful that we would one day be together again.

CHAPTER TWELVE

Early Widowhood

Often times, when I'm alone,
My thoughts are all of you.
I constantly dwell upon the past
And all that we went through.
I'll always wonder where you are
And why we are apart
Even though I know for sure
We're in each other's heart.
When you were here and in my life
We were close in every way
I guess that's why it bothers me so
To know where you are today.
Do you think of me and miss me too?
Do you wonder how I'm coping?
I can't believe you could just up and leave
Or I guess at least I'm hoping.....
That you are somewhere very near
Watching over me every day

And that someday soon we'll again be one
This is what I pray.
I love you, Bob, I always will
On that you can depend
And I'll miss you, want you and ache so to hold you
Until we meet again.
~Linda Conn 1981

FOLLOWING THE BEAUTIFUL MEMORIAL service, many guests returned to our home in Carlsbad for a personal and more intimate celebration of Bob's life. It was the first time I hosted a gathering by myself. Bob and I were big on entertaining together, so it felt strange to do it without him.

Reflecting on those early, very fresh, and tender moments shortly after Bob died, I recall how others reacted to me when they had no idea what to say in an attempt to comfort me. It all felt surreal and foreign, as if I had to learn a new way to now exist in this life.

A high school buddy of Bob's drove down from Los Angeles for the service and approached me with a big bear hug.

"Don't worry, Snookie Bear, you are young; you will meet someone again."

Though his intentions were sincere, I immediately retorted, "I'm not interested in meeting someone else...I want Bob back!"

And another well-intended comment meant to console was, "At least we know that God doesn't give us more than we can handle." I certainly was not prepared to respond to that other than to smile and nod while we hugged.

In my head, I told myself, well, God sure is pushing the envelope on this one! It is overwhelming, and I highly doubt I will ever handle it. But, eventually, I researched that promise in my Bible and found it to mean that whatever life brings our way, in this broken and imperfect world, God promises he will be there by our side to walk or carry us through. When we invite him in, he will never leave or forsake us. Over time, and literally prying my grip away from grief one finger at a time, I eventually found comfort in that verse.

Others would try to console me by saying, "He's so much better off; this is actually a blessing since he was in such pain and is no longer suffering. He's in a better place now, Linda."

Well, why was he sick in the first place? I wondered to myself. I don't want him somewhere else. The better place for him is here with me. Yet, in the end, there was simply nothing to say back.

Another favorite is "I am so sorry" unless "for your loss" is included. Ironically, I have absent-mindedly found myself saying that to others in despair, and the phrase is senseless. It brings about the question, why are you sorry? You didn't do anything. It would have been sarcastic and rude to retort that back to someone, and so far, thankfully, I have only spoken it in my head. My fake, polite self just smiled and said thank you. But thank you for what? For being sorry? You were not responsible. I was the sorry one, terribly sorry for my whole situation. It was unbearable and I did not know if I would ever climb out of it. It was more than I could fathom, more than frightening, and not where I expected to be at twenty-seven years old.

Soon, someone approached me with, "Oh I know just how you feel. My mom recently died."

Oh my gosh, I silently screamed. I know you're trying to commiserate with me, but you can't truly know how I feel unless you've been in my shoes through my journey. Maybe it would be better to say, "I can't imagine what this is like for you."

As I circled the crowd, I suddenly found myself in a group of well-meaning fellow real estate agents. To my surprise, one of them asked me if I was going to sell my house.

"I hadn't thought about that," I replied. In my mind I remember shouting, *I just buried my precious husband and have no idea if I'm going to make it through this afternoon. And you want to know if I'm going to sell our house?? Our dream home. Our haven of comfort and security. Are you kidding me???*

Once again, smiling and nodding seemed to be the only way to endure that day.

As I look back, all of these comments from those who care were, in my opinion, the most minimally comforting remarks one could make to a person who has lost a loved one. And although they sounded somewhat shallow at the time, I knew that was not their intention. They were simply meant to comfort me. But, what I've learned through this experience is that your presence is one of the most valuable ways you can show support to a grieving widow(er). Aside from "I care," "I'm here for you," or "my heart aches for you," sometimes there are no words, and silence, along with a hug, also shows love. No one can truly know how you feel or fix your situation. That is yours alone. But coming alongside, being truly available, and listening provides huge comfort to those feeling all alone and broken-hearted.

If it sounds like I was bitter, it is most likely because I was slowly entering the beginning stages of grief, and everything felt sad and scary. After learning that there was a fine line between fear and anger, I realized I teetered more toward the latter. Navigating a new and unfamiliar time in my life became my new biggest challenge.

As the afternoon fell into the evening, the broker Bob worked with and his wife made their way over to me to share their condolences. To my complete surprise, they both took my hands and said, "We would love for you to consider working with us. Bob mentioned a while back that you are a licensed agent, and we think you would be a wonderful addition to our team."

"Just think about it," they said. "We know you have a lot on your plate right now, but we have been thinking and talking a lot about this since hearing about Bob passing and couldn't wait to ask you."

I squeezed their hands and smiled as tears streamed down my cheeks. Such a gift, I thought to myself as I hung my head and nodded gratefully to both of them. All at once, I again felt fingertips on me, both God and Bob.

"Also, we are hosting a summer-end beach party in Cardiff next month, and you are more than welcome to join us. That would be a good chance for you to meet up with everyone and see how it feels."

I could not believe this was happening to me after all I had recently experienced. I suddenly saw a flicker of light, a glimmer of hope, at the end of a long, dark tunnel. But my first thought was, how could I do that without Bob? Though overwhelmed and blindsided, I did my best to muster up a response.

"I can't thank you enough—I am so honored. I will certainly consider this generous offer and be in touch," was all I could utter.

And, after all, I had nothing else going on. My life, as it were, had been completely turned upside down.

I was now a widow. A little widow, I called myself. I was too young to be a widow. I did not know how to do that. Bob and I were in his cancer battle together. I couldn't understand why he died and went to heaven, and I had to stay here and finish my life. It all seemed so unfair. I was in it with him for the long haul, and we planned to beat cancer as a team. That one person who knew this journey as I did, who was always there to support and encourage me, to cheer me on with that positive attitude and sense of humor, was no longer here. My mind whirled as I tried to imagine tackling the enormous mountain ahead.

"You are handling this with such dignity," friends marveled. I was thankful that my exterior did not reflect what my interior was experiencing, and that I could maintain the facade of coping so well. My guts were constantly churning while fear and anxiety continued to consume me. I felt like I was drowning; suffocating in my own insides; succumbing to my feelings of despair, loneliness, hopelessness, anguish, and desolation. I had lost all hope and saw very little light ahead. The flow of tears was endless and unpredictable, and the nights brought nightmares, wails, and relentless tossing and turning. It felt as though a tsunami was raging over me every single day.

After a few days, friends and family had returned to their own lives, and though I felt isolated and scared, I knew I was not truly alone. Loved ones kept a close watch on me, and God had never left my side, evident by the fact that I was still somehow managing to function. Yet when I curled up in my bed, our bed, longing for Bob's strong arms to enfold me, his lips to press upon mine, the emptiness was smothering. As I looked around the room and saw what was once our beautiful sanctuary and my dream come true, the sadness of my new reality engulfed me. Our king-size bed, once our happy place, became a massive pit of despair. Since the night Bob died, I had slept on his side to feel his presence and hopefully be able to fall asleep. I tried hard to keep my grief and loneliness at bay, but the vacancy next to me was enormous and often more than I could bear.

I gazed over at our dresser; his clothes were in the left drawers, mine in the right. It was painful to even be in our bedroom, but at the same time, it was comforting.

As I sat in his closet and breathed, inhaling his scent, a strong sense of his presence surrounded me. I will never part with these clothes, I promised myself. They were all I tangibly had left.

The enlarged framed photos of Bob from the memorial service displayed around our room were smiling at me while I wore his bathrobe, smelled his cologne, and re-read the many cards he gave me through the few years we had together. His new wedding ring was now on my left hand, next to mine. I was married to him forever.

He was not gone. He was just away for a while; he would be back, I numbly reassured myself.

As I opened our dresser doors while playing our favorite songs, my eyes honed in on his glasses, gold watch, and leather wallet, all neatly positioned. He no longer needed those things, so there they remained. I had carefully, sorrowfully placed them there after he left. I continued to absorb myself in him and fill my core with his ethereal presence, his spirit. I felt as close to him as was possible to another human being. He was the missing half of my soul.

Peering in a drawer, I noticed a sealed envelope bearing my name. As I slowly broke the seal, it was clear it was from Bob, written before he died. Did he mean to leave it there for me? Did he forget to give it to me in person? Had he intended for me to find it afterward? If I had to guess, I would say the latter. That was so like him, always thinking ahead and keeping me surprised and smiling.

But this time was not quite as exciting. I felt a sinking feeling in my stomach as I read the card. It was a beautiful love note, so typical of him. Another one to add to the collection, yet this one was different. It came after he died. He made sure of that. I was certain he planned it that way.

Looking further, I noticed the corner of a small box peeking out beneath a pair of socks. My heart was racing, my mind curiously wondering what was inside. Holding my breath, I cradled it and slowly

lifted the lid. I gasped out loud when I saw a tiny ceramic parrot brooch lying neatly on a patch of white cotton. Bob knew I adored tropical birds, and he had bought this little pin for me before he died; it was the last material gift he would ever give me. As I carefully lifted it out of the box, I wondered if he could see me from where he was now and was watching my reaction.

Instinctively, I began to talk to him as if he were there. Oh, Snookie Bear, I cried out. How precious is this! I love it, and if you were here, I would be smothering you with hugs and kisses.

With the colorful ceramic parrot clenched in my fist, I hugged my core so tight I could feel my heartbeat while embracing my spirit. I gazed upward toward the heavens and began to wail aloud, my body heaving with each mournful sob until I finally collapsed onto our bed and curled into the fetal position.

Feelings of hopelessness flooded me once again. Bob was gone. He would not be back. I knew that in my head, but my heart needed to catch up. That, I was convinced, would take a long, long time, if ever. I wondered when we would meet again and how long I would have to remain here on earth until I could return to his arms. Aside from the few cherished mementos, all I had left now were the sweet memories that could never leave me, embedded forever in my heart.

I wondered how in the world I would ever move forward from this. I awoke each day in a state of confusion and despair, and many times, for a brief moment, I allowed myself to believe it was all a bad dream. Then, as I slowly opened my eyes, reality quickly slipped back in and brought to mind the awful pain and loneliness looming ahead. Would it ever subside? How would I continue to get out of bed and escape the grief hell I was experiencing?

Moving forward, I continued to grieve and, while doing so, wondered if I was now probably supposed to be acting and living life a certain way. But who decided those rules? I didn't need to walk around in black attire, with a veil over my face, to let the world know I was grieving. Nor did I feel the need to stay home to show respect. That was probably the last thing Bob would have wanted me to do. So how does a twenty-seven-year-old know how to grieve the loss of her young husband? I knew those feelings were not soon going away and realized I needed to move through them. But I was not quite sure how to do it "properly."

My trembling hands held the card, and as I attempted to re-read it, hot tears slowly streamed down my cheeks while chills and a warm feeling wrestled in my body. Bob touched this card with his hands, I told myself. He wrote those words from his heart, knowing I would need them to move on. It was a tangible connection to him, and strangely, it provided comfort.

Even though I managed to progress a little further along each day, it often felt like I was wearing shoes filled with concrete. Frequently, I found myself frozen in a fog or haze that loomed over me, day and night, while I searched for guidance and some sense of security. Like a lonely marble in an empty box, I rolled around aimlessly, without direction or purpose. Life was carrying on around me, and I was no longer an active participant; instead, a mere observer. I was swimming in a fishbowl filled with grief. Life, as I knew it, had been ripped out from under me.

I finally pulled myself away from our room and distracted myself with the mountain of laundry awaiting me. As I loaded the machine, I came across a lone pair of boxer shorts at the bottom of the basket and realized this would be the last piece of his clothing I would ever wash. I wailed as I held them in my hands and dampened them with fresh tears. The reminders of the emptiness I felt were around every corner. I could not escape.

Eventually, the day of the beach party arrived. I spent the entire day wrestling in my mind. How could I do this alone? What would they think of me coming to a social event this soon after? Would I have anything to contribute to the conversations except tales of death and woe? I found a million excuses to stay home in my comfort zone and not force the energy I did not have. Yet somehow, deep down, I felt compelled to go and knew, in my heart, that Bob would approve. Wearing my prettiest flowery summer dress, I forced myself into the car and headed to the grocery store to pick up a bottle of wine and a bag of chips so as not to arrive empty-handed. Filled with anxiety, I headed to the beach just a few miles away. It was easy to spot the gathering from the road, but I drove past several times, back and forth along Pacific Coast Highway, until I finally forced myself to turn into the parking lot.

My body trembled while I dragged myself across the sand. But soon, I was surrounded by those who knew and loved Bob, and I was instantly folded into the group. It seemed everyone acknowledged my angst, which truly put me at ease. Before long, a couple of hours had passed while I connected with some very lovely, compassionate people.

As I drove home later that evening, with one more baby step behind me, it occurred to me that with a bit of self-prodding, and a ton of courage, I could slowly peel myself out of my despair and try new things. Being with this lively group of realtors made me feel alive, energized, and encouraged to visit their office the following week.

The next day, my brother-in-law called to check on me.

"What time did you get home last night? I tried to call, and there was no answer even after 9 pm. Where were you?"

I suddenly felt accountable yet also resentful. I did not owe Bill or anyone else any explanation about how I lived my life, and his somewhat agitated tone, wondering where I was, disturbed me. It was as if he thought he was now in charge of me and my future. Since he had come over that weekend to mow my lawn, he acted like he owned me. I knew he was hurting, too, but I was not about to let him carry on like that.

"I was invited to a party and decided to go," I told him. "I need to stay busy, or I will go crazy. It is painful to be in this house without Bob, especially at night."

At the end of the call, I knew he was unhappy, but that was not my problem.

Monday morning arrived with a fresh thought.

There was a reason I was still here, and I needed to discover that purpose. I had to find a new meaning in my life.

I forced myself out of bed to take on the new day.

You have to be tough, Linda. So I pushed myself to try.

My sales license was still active and I knew I needed to go back to work, so I finally mustered up the courage to go to the office and explore the new opportunity, knowing that would be what Bob would want me to do. How Bob would have handled it became my new mantra.

When I tentatively walked through the office door, his broker immediately jumped up and greeted me with a big hug.

"I am so glad to see you, Linda," he smiled. "I think you are going to enjoy working with our group."

He took me through the office and introduced me to those I had not yet met while other familiar faces greeted me with warm handshakes and hugs. To be so welcomed felt amazing. As we walked across the room toward the desk I had come to visit many times before, a sharp pang of anguish cut me to the core. Little did I know that the desk Bob had occupied would become mine, left just as it was before he died. I suddenly felt his presence around me and wondered if he had a hand in this.

Drawing a deep breath, I slowly sat down in his chair and gradually began to open his desk drawers. Inside were his scratchpads and files filled with his writing, neatly arranged next to his appointment book, sparse with entries. Suddenly my eye caught a glimpse of his coffee mug with a not-too-old tea stain on the bottom. I picked up the cup, held it close to my chest, traced my finger over the edge, and then pressed it to my lips. His lips had once touched that mug—those lips I will never again kiss here on this earth—and I longed to drink him in and hold him close to me forever.

Though sweet memories remained deep in my heart, the ache and yearning for more created an unbearable raw, open wound. I had to get away. I could not do this. Fear and panic overwhelmed me, and quickly, without looking at anyone, I hurried out of the office, jumped into my car, and returned to my safety zone…our bedroom…now my bedroom.

Once again, I asked myself how I would ever do this. As if on a timer, the tears streamed softly down my cheeks while I consoled myself that I had another big day under my belt. I knew the only way to make it was to keep going through it, one day, one step, one minute at a time. Yet, I just wanted to curl up in a ball until it was over. The pain was too much to face. I did not want to go down that road alone, yet I knew I was not alone. I was moving one step forward, two steps back. It felt like my own personal board game and, for some reason, I was bound and determined to win.

A photo of Bob wearing his bright green scrubs caught my attention one evening while glancing through one of our photo albums. Where he got them, I could not recall. He found them for a Halloween party when we were newly married, but he continued to wear them as pajamas, especially in the hospital. I had embroidered his name on the top and bottom—in bright orange thread—which made them very personal. The picture reminded me that I had only the bottoms. After he passed away, he was wearing only the top when the mortuary wheeled him out on the gurney.

A few days later, I went to the mortuary to retrieve the green top, only to find out they had destroyed it. I was angry, sad, and hurt. With tears burning in my eyes, I took my anger and despair out on them and, in addition, told them they should get rid of the 'we take credit cards' signs so clearly displayed in their funeral parlor showroom. It made everything seem so commercial, like the business that it was. I detested them. They also discarded the pillow Rocky had placed under his head. That was so cruel. I wanted to take those things home, hold them, breathe them in, and feel his presence forever. They were gone now. Feeling forlorn, betrayed, and abandoned, I scurried away from the mortuary and walked slowly up the hill to his still fresh gravesite, where I sat and cried.

But time did move on, though I frequently found myself spinning out of control with regrets and guilt. I often wondered what might have happened if we had pursued a second opinion about the initial hemorrhoid diagnosis earlier. Would they have detected cancer sooner, and would Bob still be alive? Agonizing over that notion, I continued to self-blame and constantly beat myself up for things I could not change. But why did I not insist upon it in the first place?

And then I relived that awful day when Bob called me to come and lie next to him after I had given him yet another pain injection and had rushed out of the room feeling depressed and afraid. We had been having so much difficulty dealing with his pain and my inability to control it. Although I had only taken a moment to catch a breath and turn on *I Love*

Lucy, I saturated myself with self-imposed guilt. Feelings of inadequacy consumed me, yet it was so not about me.

I tried to imagine what that brief moment must have been like for him, lying there alone, and regret again devoured me. I had allowed fear to prevail back then as I panicked about what was ahead, all of the unknowns that lingered right around the corner. I was only twenty-seven, with so much life still ahead of me. I could not make sense of any of it.

But Bob was equally young and undoubtedly wondered the same, if not more. His was the life in jeopardy, and although there were many unanswered questions, it did not matter; it was clearly out of our control. Yet, ultimately, we both trusted God. It was his plan, not ours. I consoled myself that I was only human and bound to have a moment here and there when I needed to regroup. It was all just so overwhelming for both of us.

Shortly after Bob died, my sister, Sandy, asked me if it would be helpful if she moved in with me. I was not only in complete shock that she would suggest this, but I was more than grateful for the support and protection she was willing to offer me during her young life. She was only twenty-three and had been enjoying college life away at San Diego State University.

I have to believe now that this offer was somewhat pre-planned on her part. She was not only worried about me but also had an unfortunate situation happen that I was unaware of until after Bob passed.

When Bob became ill, Sandy was dating one of his friends, whose dad was a pathologist. Shortly after his first surgery, the father took it upon himself to review the pathology report and affirmed a dismal prognosis for Bob, which he shared with his son and my sister. HIPPA laws did not exist at that time.

Sandy, to this day, still has much angst about this, as she had to acknowledge that possible truth yet keep it from me for two long years to protect Bob and me and preserve our hope. Recently, however, Sandy and I spoke about that regrettable predicament. We both concluded that God was preparing her for what was ahead, and she thus rearranged her life to be there for me. What a blessing!

I doubt I would have survived those early days of grief had my sister not been there with me in that house after Bob was gone. As difficult as it was for her to live with that information, it ultimately played out for good. I continue to marvel at things that happen that I do not get or understand initially, only to see the fruit much later. It is truly astounding.

In the initial days after Bob died, when I was trying to figure out who I was and attempting to go back to work, it took everything I had to get up in the morning and make myself move forward. I had little energy and zero desire to get out of bed. If it weren't for a dear friend, Kevin, who I met from Bob's, and now my, real estate office, I don't know how I would have made it. He would ring me early in the morning to see if I was up and then make me promise that I would meet him at the office. He was a godsend.

A couple of months after Bob died, I was in Los Angeles having lunch with an old friend of my father-in-law, and afterward, I decided to stop by Cedars-Sinai. Longing to feel his presence, I aimlessly wandered the seventh floor and mentally and emotionally revisited the times we were there, full of hope and optimism. It was eerie to walk down the familiar hallways, past the nursing station, and peer reminiscently into those rooms where we had spent so many weeks and built so many bittersweet memories.

As I was leaving the hospital, crossing over the long bridge from one tower to the other to get to the parking lot, I surprisingly ran into Dr. Sherman. It was shocking to see him at first, but at the same time, quite comforting.

After exchanging a hug, I ultimately had to ask him about that Friday when Bob and I came to his office. "Why did you choose not to see us for our final appointment?"

"I remember that day very well and cannot tell you how sorry I am, Linda. I could not bear to face the two of you. I knew you had some very pointed questions, and the probable truth would have been devastating. So I decided not to address them."

As tears welled in my eyes, I looked up at him and, barely above a whisper, asked, "So why did you not tell us the truth before it came to that point?"

"I didn't want to take away your hope," he told me. "You two were always so optimistic and positive, and since I am not God, I did not feel it was right for me to say anything that would possibly deprive you of that. Hope was all you two had left."

He gently put his hand on my shoulder as I hung my head.

"Thank you for caring so much about us. Please tell me how you do this day after day?" I asked him.

"I have a wife like you by my side," he said.

With that familiar lump in my throat, I turned my face toward his and softly smiled. I will never forget what he said and what it meant to me. He validated me when I was feeling so uncertain and consumed with guilt. Whenever I wondered if I could have done better caring for Bob, Dr. Sherman's words healed that for me. He assured me that I had done all I could. Our conversation was a significant turning point in restoring my confidence and belief in myself and created a definite positive step forward in the grief process. I walked away feeling a bit lighter and greatly comforted by his words. The grace I received that day helped restore me.

Soon, another hurdle was on the horizon, my first Christmas without Bob. The holidays were always a magical time for us, and the thought of facing them without him filled me with anticipation, anxiety, and dread. I could not imagine how I would make it through.

A few weeks before the holiday season arrived, I instinctively knew I needed to plan something different that year for his brother, sister, and me to escape the void left by Bob's death. The holidays without him would be a challenge for all of us, another jolt of reality, so we needed to create a new tradition. I felt responsible for that and for them.

One evening the three of us and Sandy were having dinner together at my house when I raised my glass in a toast.

"Here's to health, happiness, and all the right decisions!"

We all cheered and laughed as we thought about our fearless leader and felt his strength envelop us.

"I've been thinking about Christmas this year and came up with an idea I wanted to run by you guys," I shared excitedly.

"How about we all drive up to Big Bear and spend Christmas Eve skiing the slopes?"

The faces around the table lit up, and everyone was happily on board. We chatted light-heartedly about that idea and how fun it would be. It felt great to be together in our grief and eventual healing.

In early December, my real estate office was having a Christmas party and the thought of attending it made me feel anxious. I knew I needed to go, but I didn't want to go alone. And I did not feel it was appropriate to go with one of the guys from the office, only four months after Bob passed. One day, my cousin Rick was visiting and I asked if he would mind taking me to the party. He gladly accepted and it was the perfect solution. His presence made the evening comfortable and easy, which helped me overcome one more tiny hurdle.

Two weeks before Christmas, my dad called to tell me that my Papa had suffered a fatal heart attack. It was Sunday evening, and he had been watching *60 Minutes* on TV with my grandma and eating an ice cream cone; the next minute he was gone. I was devastated. My Papa, whom I adored and was so close to, was no longer there. In less than one year, my family had lost three prominent men—my Uncle Dick, Bob, and now my Papa. It was painful to think of life without them.

With perfect timing, Christmas Eve arrived, and at the crack of dawn, I drove us up to the mountains to carry out our new tradition. Our favorite tunes were playing as we sang our way to the top. It was a beautiful day, the sun glistened on the freshly fallen powder, and it was noticeably uncrowded when we pulled into the lodge parking lot.

After renting our equipment and downing a quick hot chocolate, we glided to the nearest chairlift to enjoy our first ride down the snow-packed mountain.

"This is the perfect day," I declared. "Woo hoo!"

The conditions could not have been better; the winter scenery was glorious.

While waiting in line, we all laughed as we imagined how Bob would feel about our crazy decision to do something entirely different to celebrate Christmas Eve.

"You know he would be all for this," his brother said, smiling, while holding a thumbs-up.

We all concurred that he would indeed approve and that, from afar, he was most likely encouraging us to make the most of it.

Nearing the next chair, I suddenly heard a familiar voice close by, and just before approaching my seat turned around to see who it was. My eyes had to be playing tricks on me. Bob's surgeon, Dr. Sherman, was directly behind me with his family. The man who did everything he could to help my husband stay alive in his battle with cancer was now just behind me in the ski lift line, atop the mountain where I was trying to escape from the reality of it all.

How was that possible? What were the odds of that happening? I was happy to see him, of course, and he was warm and welcoming to me, as always. It suddenly felt like only a blip away from our time together when Bob was still with us. But deep down, I wondered about the meaning of this and if Bob had a hand in it. How would I ever be able to disconnect myself from him and all we had experienced while these situations continued to occur? And, honestly, did I really want to be or feel disconnected?

My personal belief in all of this was that there were no coincidences. God knew that would happen; I needed to reflect, accept and make peace with it and continue pursuing the beginning of my new life. I felt the presence of Bob and God and ultimately believed that both were condoning our little getaway trip. And nearly forty years later, I realize the hope those encounters gave me along the way, as they helped me re-establish my own life. There was clearly something more, and I knew I needed to keep moving forward to find out what was ahead.

CHAPTER THIRTEEN

Grief and Building a New Life

IMMERSING DEEPER INTO THE grief I was already experiencing, trying to survive alone became my new norm in life. And dealing with those issues back in the 1980s was quite a challenging journey.

A few months into the process, my sister recommended a therapist for me to visit and receive some grief guidance. Unfortunately, counseling was not a popular concept at the time and proved unhelpful for me in moving forward. Meeting with the therapist in our initial session was troublesome.

"Give me a little background about what is going on for you," he said.

Inhaling a deep breath, I recounted the last two years of my life when Bob was ill and after his passing.

"I'm feeling very low lately, with almost zero ambition to move ahead and unsure of what I should do with myself. It is hard to force myself out of bed. I have been working, which gives me a sense of purpose, but the real estate market is plummeting, and I am not feeling very successful or secure."

He paused, looked at me, and said, "I sense a flat affect in you and a low level of emotion. There are five steps in pushing through grief, and you seem to be in the depression and denial stages. Shock is repressing your emotions, keeping you numb." Really? I thought to myself. And I am paying how much for this? I had already read the only book on grief available then, *On Death and Dying*, by Elizabeth Kubler Ross, and I was well aware of the current thinking on the grief process.

"I suggest that you get out more, start dating, and see if that might help. Since you are so young, that should not be difficult. You might also want to make an appointment with your medical doctor to request medication, perhaps Valium." He made a few more notes and comments before sending me on my way.

As I mentioned, grief therapy was a new concept, and it took one visit for me to realize it would not help me. I was not about to start taking a habit-forming drug for something I hoped would end long before I could overcome a newly developed drug addiction.

But I heeded his advice about making an appointment with my family doctor, for peace of mind if nothing else. Dr. Miller had seen Bob and me over the past two years, so he was familiar with our situation.

"How are you doing, Linda?" he asked when he saw me. "I was so sorry to hear that Bob passed. I imagine this must be such a difficult time in your life."

I immediately choked up, and while he examined me, I shared my despair.

"I am so lonely, Dr. Miller. I have no idea how I will ever pull out of this and feel normal again."

After the exam, he asked me to meet him in his office, which I did. As I sat across the desk from him, a man well into his fifties, I could not believe what he said next.

"I am going to prescribe birth control for you, Linda. You are so young, and I think it would be helpful for you to start dating and have sex."

I was devastated when he handed me a script for a diaphragm and wished me well. As I drove home, feeling more confused than ever, the tears poured down my cheeks while I thought about all I had lost in such a short period. I was not one to go out and have casual sex and was offended that he would suggest that. It seemed that no one knew how to counsel a young widow.

A high school friend of Bob's visited from Los Angeles later that evening to take me to dinner. When I shared my recent experiences with him and mentioned that the doctor gave me birth control, he immediately perked up and said, with a sly smile, "I am happy to help you with that."

I blew him off with a chuckle, but inside I was mortified. I realized I had become a vulnerable creature on which to prey. Lovemaking, once precious and sacred to my marriage, now held no value. The well-intended advice and feedback I received were not working for me. And to further complicate things, several of our previous couple friends began to avoid me. I assumed and later discovered the truth: that married women worried that their husbands would be compelled to try and help me since I was a young widow. I involuntarily became labeled as a threat. I fell into bed that night in a heap of hopelessness and feared what might come next.

Shortly after Bob passed, Ray began spending much time with me. He was married, and he and his wife were our longtime friends. I was comfortable with him and appreciated his suggestions and helpful nature. But things soon began to take a turn; he started courting me.

I arrived home one afternoon from a weekend in Palm Springs with my sister to find the walkway to my front door lined with baskets of beautiful flowers. Additionally, a handwritten note was lying on my front porch. "I love you, Linda. Ray." I was flattered but dismissed it as I knew he was also grieving.

Yet when he took me to lunch to discuss my finances and other issues to help me move forward, the conversation frequently turned to his feelings for me. Then he began to talk about marriage. I was blindsided and felt very uncomfortable whenever we were with each other.

"You are a married man, Ray," I would tell him. "We are friends and nothing more."

But he continued to pursue me and even walked me by a jewelry store one day after lunch to see if there was a ring I liked.

I was exhausted just being a widow, and now I had a whole other scenario challenging me. I never wished to hurt him, but I could not continue like this. Though my boundaries were on full alert, I was weary and vulnerable, which concerned me. And since we held some real estate investments together, I knew I needed to have a delicate conversation with him.

"Ray, I appreciate your feelings for me and all the help and support you have given since Bob died. Your friendship is invaluable, but this can't continue. As long as you are married, I'm not available to you. I do not do that."

"Well, darling, if you say you will marry me, I will get a divorce."

"That's not how it works, Ray. I am not even sure how I feel, and I would never break up a marriage to find out."

Ray suddenly became frustrated with me.

"It is so unfair what Bob did to you," his eyes filled with hurt. "He spoiled you with cards, flowers, and an over-abundance of love, making it difficult for anyone to ever measure up."

I took into consideration what he was saying, especially for my future encounters, but he didn't seem to understand that what he was asking of me was not at all possible.

The awkwardness grew heavy, and getting together was no longer the same. I made sure my sister or cousins were with us when we connected. Otherwise, it was far too unpleasant for me.

Meanwhile, working in the real estate office while still in my twenties afforded me many opportunities to meet people, men included. I found those who paid me any attention intriguing, especially those who knew Bob. It was somehow comforting.

The first man I connected with was a fellow realtor in my new office. We decided to keep our situation confidential; for me, it seemed way too soon to date, and for him, it felt weird and wrong courting the widow his friend left behind. Since we wanted to avoid judgment from others, we stayed under the radar as much as possible. Because he knew Bob, he was comfortable talking with me about him, his illness, and subsequent death. Soon, I began to accept his and others' invitations to go out to dinner, but it seemed that all I talked about was Bob, his death, and my grief. I also realized I was becoming highly critical, comparing everyone I met to Bob.

Bob would never say or do that, I would tell myself. As more time passed, his pedestal grew higher and higher until I finally realized what I was doing. I forced myself to bring him down a notch or two by recalling imperfect instances and reminding myself of an argument we had that ended with him sleeping on the couch. That exercise helped me recognize that Bob and our relationship were not as perfect as I remembered. It was difficult to reflect on the negatives, but necessary in order to move forward. I needed to stop idolizing him. It was truly unfair to others and, at the same time, held me back from moving on.

* * *

One Saturday evening in the spring, nearing the end of my first year of grief, Sandy and I went on a sunset cruise on San Diego Bay. It was a singles event she had found and encouraged me to join. I was glad she did, as I met an intriguing man who invited me to dinner the following week. Our time together was nice enough, but when he walked me to my front door afterward, he looked around and said, "Well, I see that you got the house," assuming I was divorced.

After all that I had endured, his comment hit me sideways.

"Yeah, I got the house all right, and I got his clothes, too. Would you like to see them?" My hurt was blaring.

He immediately apologized and scurried away. Once again, it became clear how difficult it was to be a young widow.

* * *

I concluded that I needed to embrace this new phase of my life and become a new person, someone enjoyable and fascinating to be around. I needed to reinvent myself. Creating a list of goals—physically, emotionally, spiritually, financially, and socially—helped me think about what I wanted in life and what I needed to do to be successful. It was kind of like creating a roadmap for my future. So by the end of the first year of grief, I was slowly moving into a new phase and beginning to feel a little more whole.

On a gloomy June morning, nearly a year after Bob died, Sandy and I were having coffee when she said to me, "Have you ever thought of moving from this house and starting over somewhere fresh and new?"

"I had not thought of that," I told her with a look of surprise. "I guess it never occurred to me that I could make a change."

Once she said it, though, the wheels in my head began to turn. I had three mortgages on our home, and the real estate market was not making me rich. I felt instant relief at the thought of getting out from under it all. Additionally, I was in a residential neighborhood occupied by young couples and their children, scattered with strollers and tricycles, a constant reminder of my broken dreams.

It felt like freedom as I allowed myself to explore other options. So, after much more thought and input from those I trusted, I listed my home for sale. To my surprise, our friend Kevin from my office sold it in two weeks. Considering how depressed the market was, I did well. The only stressful issue was that the buyers were paying cash, and they wanted to take possession in two weeks.

As I looked around our beautiful home, I was overwhelmed by the closets and drawers full of clothes, his and mine, a double garage loaded floor to ceiling with his tools, workbench, and all the treasures we had collected during our short time together. I wondered how I would ever get it done. But with blind faith, I signed the contract and began to pack up my married life in an attempt to start over.

Friends and family rallied and helped me sort through the various piles of keep, giveaway, and unsure. By the end of the second week, I was just about to wrap it up. I secured a nearby storage unit and loaded it with the things I wanted to keep… and those with which I could not quite part. A friend in my office mentioned she needed to find a tenant for her condo for just one month, starting right at the close of my escrow, so my sister and I camped there. It was the perfect landing spot until we found a more permanent place.

* * *

Two twenty-something-year-old single girls living in a condo overlooking the seventh green on the golf course in La Costa were footloose and fancy free. Moving from our home helped me release the daily reminders and memories that held me back. I felt like I was sprung from a cannon into a new life, enabling me to continue my quest to become a fresh and fascinating person. With Sandy entirely on board, we set sail on new adventures, including meeting and dating some eligible, single men.

* * *

Although the major ordeal of selling our dream home and relocating my 'stuff' at the end of my first year alone was a step in the right direction, it certainly didn't take away the grief I had yet to deal with. It was simply that—a relocation—but it was somewhat refreshing, moving to a totally new and neutral location. The interim condo, not far from the beach, albeit only a one bedroom, was spacious.

"How do you feel about taking over the living room?" I asked my sister. She gladly agreed to camp out there while I took the master suite. The only downside was that pets were not allowed so I had to make the tough decision to part with my beloved Brandie. That thought had crossed my mind more than once during the year following Bob's passing, as I had a feeling my life was about to become busier and more complicated, not affording me the time to give Brandie the attention she deserved and was accustomed to getting. In fact, during one of my many visits to see Rocky and Esther in Washington, we discussed the possibility of Brandie moving up there and being adopted by them. As much as this was a lot to ask, they were willing to do anything that would enable me to move forward.

Soon after we made this decision, I bought a crate and a cargo ticket and drove my sweet dog, along with a couple of her favorite toys, to Lindbergh Field, where she boarded a Seattle-bound plane.

Brandie had brought so much joy and life to Bob and me, during some very challenging and sad times. She was our baby—the baby we never conceived together—and this difficult situation triggered some poignant memories.

* * *

One cold, rainy Sunday evening, when Bob was feeling extremely miserable, Brandie, after I let her out for her nightly potty, promptly jumped our backyard fence and took off in the dark. I left Bob in bed hoping his recent pain shot would soon take effect, grabbed a flashlight and umbrella, donned a raincoat and began my neighborhood search. As I worked my way around our cul-de-sac whisper-yelling her name, *Brandie!* I could see that the nearby trash cans, all set out on the street for the next day's pickup, had been rummaged and rooted through—one by one—obviously by an excited little dog on a mission. Luckily, I had also grabbed some rubber gloves when I ran out the door, and as I cleaned up all of our neighbors' trash, I was not saying very nice things under my breath about Brandie.

"You little shit," I thought. "Isn't my life hard enough right now— why are you making it so much more difficult?" Finally, when I found her on her sixth barrel of trash diggings, she reeked. I scooped her up, took her home, and threw her into the tub. As quietly as I could, I washed and rinsed her until the stench dissipated. And then she promptly, and happily, crawled under our bed covers with her humans and went sound to sleep. I laid awake silently wondering how I was doing all of this... and how long I could continue.

* * *

Yet, as I watched her little carrier move forward on the conveyor belt, her scared brown eyes staring at me, I let go of the tears I had been suppressing. At the same time, I reminded myself that yes, this was hard, but not nearly as difficult and painful as watching my beloved husband be lowered twelve feet into the ground nearly one year prior.

Bob and Brandie in earlier, healthy days

Sadness, grief, endings,   and prioritizing the severity of my losses were my new normals now; somehow I knew I would get through this change also. Everything was relative in comparison.

Sometime during my first year of grief, a strong and very powerful oppressive cloud came over me, commonly known as survivor's guilt. As a result, it became more and more difficult to enjoy each new day and event that came my way without experiencing an element of guilt for still being here on earth, and being able to take pleasure in all that this life had to offer. Why me? Why was I still here while Bob, at his very young age, had to transition to heaven for the next phase of his life? I struggled to combat this horrible, self-imposed feeling of disloyalty on my part, but more often than not found myself succumbing to remorse and regret that I was alive and he wasn't; I was left to continue and supposedly enjoy life, and in some ways it felt like a betrayal to him. My life was empty without him.

Since the beginning of my life without Bob was filled with grief, confusion, and a blanket of numbness, it's no surprise that it wasn't until our first Christmas a few months after his death, on the ski slope, that the guilt began to rear its ugly head. I tried hard not to let it squelch the forced joy I was longing to feel, but as soon as I saw Bob's surgeon on the mountain, the pangs of remorse were there to stay. The blatant reminder that I was out having fun—and Bob wasn't—was almost more than I could bear. However, once I recognized this, it later became easier to catch myself before it consumed me.

The second year of grief was now upon me and one would have thought life would become easier. Not that I expected my up and down feelings of despair to magically disappear, but at the very least, I had hoped they would lessen. Yet most anyone who has experienced deep loss will tell you that the second year is often even harder than the first. Perhaps the expectation that I should be on the mend by now was a setup for disappointment. We think we've cried all the tears, felt all the emotions, done all the work, and now life should surely fall back into place with a new normal. For me, the burning desire to hear Bob's voice, see his smile, and kiss his lips became increasingly unbearable as time away from him grew longer. I missed everything about him and tried desperately to fill the huge voids in my life resulting from his death.

Not only had I lost my spouse, best friend, soulmate, confidant, and lover, but also my lifelong fairy-tale dream, my job, my financial/decision-making partner, and, ultimately, my identity. Who was I now? Who was I to become? I was no longer a wife, a teammate, a caregiver.

In spite of all that, I was still alive and filled with all of the desires of a young woman. I longed to be married for the rest of my life. I yearned for a family and a 'normal' life with the man of my dreams. What the heck had happened?

Back in those days, one only had books to rely on and there were very few written on bereavement. But, as was previously mentioned, the stages of grief were made very clear in Elizabeth Kubler Ross's guide *On Death and Dying*. That book made me mindful each day of where I stood and gave me hope that I'd soon progress on to the next stages and finally get to the end. Yet I found myself all over the board, moving from sadness to anger to guilt to denial and then back to sadness again. I learned, from personal experience, that this model wasn't necessarily linear, and it was more normal to move in and out of each stage and repeat randomly. My grief was so unpredictable that I would often find myself bursting into tears over the very smallest thing. For example, I could be in the grocery store and a familiar song would come on. If it reminded me at all of Bob and the love we shared, I lost it. One time I remember leaving my half-filled cart in the middle of an aisle and racing out to my car. My emotions were scattered all over the place. Even though my brain kept telling me I needed to move along and inch forward, my heart was not in sync. I didn't think I'd ever pull myself out of the depressing, confusing mire in which I was immersed.

"I'll never do that again," I told a good friend one day. "Getting so attached to someone and giving your heart away is extremely risky and it is way too painful if they leave you."

"But, Linda, if you choose that attitude and never take another risk, you're not living life," he said to me. That comment stayed with me and to this day still helps guide me when I feel stuck.

Thus, it seemed that the only way to accomplish those new goals of mine was to get out there and start doing just what my friend said… live life. At first, I have to admit, the thought of dating another man felt very odd and wrong, like I was being unfaithful to Bob. But then I heard a wise quote that helped spring me forward: "It is a compliment to your deceased spouse to want to marry again. It only means that your lives together were happy times and you want that back." And I was fortunate that Bob had actually encouraged me to do so before he died. Most of all, being married to Bob had given me faith in relationships and marriage, and my ultimate desire was to find that happy place again. So I realized I didn't need to feel guilty for feeling that way. Instead, I felt hopeful that there was more life ahead of me.

CHAPTER FOURTEEN

Reflecting and Moving On

"Hope is not pretending that troubles don't exist... It is the trust that they will not last forever, and that hurts will be healed and difficulties overcome... or at least managed... with time."
~Author Unknown

ON SO MANY LEVELS, my life was fragmented and not at all the fairy tale I was promised long ago when I believed that if I met my prince, all of my dreams would come true. And although I was becoming a completely different person, I was still the woman I had always been and needed to stay true to myself and my life values. I thought back to a character in my childhood, a cheerful, singing cricket, who advised me to always let my conscience guide me. That was becoming a challenge for me, given what society and professionals were advising me to do. When I met Bob, I was a virgin, so the thought of being with anyone else was overwhelming. Yet, although I longed to feel alive again, the advice on how to make that happen mystified me. My conscience was confused.

Thus, I continued to work on myself and my new status. Not only did I begin to date, I met a couple of men who seemed interesting.

Additionally, John, Bob's childhood friend, kept in touch with me, as any best friend would. He was with me when Bob passed and was now away at medical school, but he faithfully checked on me via phone or snail mail. Because John was familiar and safe, my feelings for him grew, but I knew I needed to keep that in check as he was married. At least I found out my heart was still working and slowly coming back to life.

Returning to school, I pursued my passion of becoming a nurse, taking classes in the evening. And I eventually left the downward-spiraling real estate field for a more secure, full-time position where I could utilize my skills to manage the office of a local builder.

Jogging at the beach became my new form of outdoor exercise; it was a healthy outlet and a great physical release, and it allowed me to feel closer to Bob as I looked out on the horizon. Many times I would wander down to the coast at sunset, and while the giant ball of fire sank slowly into the ocean, I could almost envision heaven. I often found myself talking to Bob in hopes he could hear me.

"I hope you are okay up there," I would whisper to the skyline. "You'll never know how hard this is without you and how much I miss you."

Somehow that made me feel better inside, yet at the same time, often brought me to tears. But as life moved forward, the tears came less and less as the pain decreased. Bob slowly became a sweet memory—one that would remain in my heart forever.

My sister invited me to join her gym, where I tried an aerobic dancing class for the first time. I loved it so much that I went out and bought a cute leotard and some high-top Reeboks and began to attend classes at least three times a week. Doing so made me feel alive.

I also applied for and was approved as a volunteer Big Sister to a young girl needing a role model. Rebecca was thirteen; her mother was a single mom who worked full-time and needed extra support for her daughter during that critical, impressionable age. I delighted in taking her on outings after school, and we enjoyed long talks and time together. It was a win-win.

Continuing to journal, I kept track of my progress in each area of my life, noting things I needed to improve upon, and when I looked back, I could see how far I had come. Those decisions were necessary and satisfying while I tried to stay healthy in all those important areas: physically, emotionally, spiritually, financially, and socially. It felt like I was gradually creating a new me, putting the broken pieces back together and producing a fully revised blueprint.

Surrounding myself with as much security as possible—including moving in with family, maintaining a steady income, clinging to relatives and friends, and working on my positive attitude—I plodded forward and tackled this unfamiliar territory. Spending special moments with my young cousins, Katrina and Rob, helped me with my longing for children. We spent countless hours together doing sleepovers at their house and mine, going to the park, church, movies, the beach, and other fun-filled

Linda "Deda", Katrina, Rob, and Brandie

activities. These precious little ones filled an emptiness looming within me, since I had no children of my own.

A couple of other therapeutic exercises during my time of deep grief included repeating my story to anyone who would listen; it was another step toward healing the broken dreams of my life. I found that sharing my emotions somewhat lessened the pain. Additionally, I periodically wrote to Bob as a way to stay connected. I loved updating him on my life and the changes since he died. Nearing the second anniversary of his passing, I wrote him the following letter:

Hi Bob!

Do you remember me—your Snookie Bear? I sure do miss you a lot. What's it like where you are now? It sure is lonely here without you. I can't even begin to tell you how much and how many people miss you and the influence you left on the lives you touched. You wouldn't believe it! I'm so proud of you, Bob, and how lucky was I to be your wife. You were, without a doubt, the best husband and friend I could ever hope for. I'm so thankful to have shared the few years we had together but sad that the last two had to be so painful for you. I know you're in a much better place now and finally relieved of your pain and suffering. God knows you did your share here and you'll never, ever know how much I admire the strength and courage you showed through the absolute worst of times.

I often think about your final weekend and how incredible that must have been for you, Bob. What were you thinking each time one of your friends came to visit you? Well, I discussed this with Paige, Dr. Sherman's nurse, once I knew what was going to happen, and asked her what or how you would feel about all of your "long-lost" friends and family coming in and out of our room to see you for possibly the last time. She assured me I was doing the right thing and that seeing all of your closest people would be a gift to you. I often ponder now what was going on in your mind during that time. You were pretty heavily sedated—I was making sure of that—but I know you must have realized something was up. I mean—my gosh—all in one week Rocky and Esther came from Seattle, John, his brother Chris, and our other friend Rocky flew in from CT, Marty and other friends from Los Angeles you hadn't seen in forever, plus everyone else who lived nearby—you must have wondered something right? Our house was filled with our loved ones.

And I think it's so neat that you and I never really faced your death or allowed ourselves to truly believe that you actually were going to soon transcend from this life to another. I hope you know that when I had to tell you what Dr. Sherman "laid on me" one week before you died—"that you were going to die and I was about to witness what it is like to die of cancer"—was so hard for me to deal with alone, without you. Thank God Ray was with me.

But soon after, I knew I needed to share that with you. Since we never kept any secrets from each other why start now? It was clear to me that once you knew the truth, it would make it easier for you to make the transition you inevitably had to make and I remember when I did tell you that you were going to die—can you even imagine that Bob?—it felt like we were finally sharing the all-time 'secret' that we had never wanted to think or talk about. And when I watched as your eyes opened wide I realized that you knew I was telling you the truth and the rest was pretty much up to you. And please believe me when I tell you that *it took all of my courage to tell you this—the hardest thing I've ever done—and you handled it so well, lover.*

Only a few hours later you peacefully transcended from life with "us" to the new and hopefully exciting unknown world ahead of you. What were you feeling then? Did you know that I was there by your side and held onto you while you took your last painful breath? I can honestly tell you I felt relieved for you—no more pain, no more injections, no more wondering what was next.

And now I can't possibly express to you how much I miss you and how lonely life is here without you. In a way, I'm glad you don't have to endure all that is involved in living life without your buddy, your soulmate. It's a real drag, lover, and believe me, I'll never (and I know I shouldn't say never) meet a man like you again and I also realize how very fortunate I was to be married to you. This has been a sad and empty journey without you here to walk it with me. Yet I'm grateful for the huge cluster of family and friends you left behind, who have bonded even closer as a result of your death. You were always looking out for me.

I'm trying so hard to carry on—as you would have done. I love you, Bob, and I always will.

- Your Snookie Bear

Reflecting on that letter made me realize how attached I had been to Bob and also how dependent I was, which now felt a bit frightening. Somewhere deep in my spirit, probably because I'd moved in with Bob from my parents' home, I knew I needed to challenge myself to live alone, and prove to myself that I could do it.

So I forced myself to move away from my sister and my aunt, with whom I lived during that second year, and I rented a short-term place nearby. I had an intuition that one day I might need to fall back on that experience.

During that six-month interval, I improved my credit, increased my savings account, and thus the ability to qualify for a loan, so I began to shop for a condo. After locating the perfect place, I moved in when my lease was up. And fortunately, a few weeks later, my sister again joined me.

In that next season, the beginning of the third year, I experienced much growth, change, self-confidence, and ultimately the desire to grow in a forward direction. It was also time for me to once again communicate with Bob through my writing:

Dearest Bob,

My life seems so empty
Since you went away
Oftentimes I've wondered
How I'll make it through each day.

I think about you all the time
Even though it's been three years
The pain I feel seems never ending
I can't stop the flow of tears.

I've had to totally re-build my life
It's so different without you, Bob.
I've moved, returned to school, made new friends
Even have a full-time job.

Oh I've dated some, here and there
And even felt like I was in love;
But how can it ever be like it was with us
When YOU are somewhere up above?

I try so hard not to compare
And realize I have changed
But each time I meet someone new
I end up feeling so strange.

No one can make me feel like you did, Bob
You loved me with all of your heart.
I long for your arms to hold me close
And for you to say we'll never again be apart.

But I must go on, I'm still so young
My own life's journey is yet to come.
Keep watch over me and guide me, Bob,
until God calls me home.

I long to meet someone who loves me like you do
And with him raise a family.
If God does give me another chance at love
I will cherish him until eternity.

~ Linda Conn, 1984

Life did move on, whether I was ready or not. And time, as they say, does help heal. It was clear that the time had come for me to get over that

fantasy notion; to realize, and eventually accept the reality, the truth...
Bob was gone, and my life with him here on earth was over. He was not
coming back.

It was around this time that I made the decision to permanently
remove my wedding ring from my left hand. I had intermittently taken
it off, but quickly slid it back on whenever I felt sad, lonely, or scared. It
somehow provided comfort and security in my ever-changing world. But
it suddenly seemed appropriate and natural to take this big step in order
to launch myself forward in my new life.

Now settled into my new home, new job, and forever-changed
identity, I awoke one Saturday morning feeling like a bear coming out
of winter hibernation. The warm sunshine blazed through my bedroom
window and new life was staring me in the face. It was the end of
summer, and I was pleased with where I now was in my life—physically,
emotionally, spiritually, financially, and socially. Those important areas
had suffered after Bob died, but now, three years later, they felt cohesive
and much more solid.

As I walked out to the kitchen to pour a cup of coffee, my sister
Sandy slowly sauntered in from her bedroom.

"You seem perky this morning," she said as she grabbed a mug and
joined me in the dining room, still in our jammies. "Did you have a good
sleep?"

I was literally beaming when I told her I was ready to move on. That
was a huge step for me.

"Yes, I slept great and somehow I'm feeling different today—a lot
like my old self."

"That's great Linda! Why do you think that is?"

"I guess just feeling more settled and secure has brought me back to
a place of 'normalcy.' And it feels great, by the way. Hey—it's Saturday,"

I said, "what are you doing tonight?" I knew her current boyfriend was away on a military assignment, and she might be available.

"No plans," she said. "What do you have in mind?"

"Well, Cindy and Jim mentioned that they might want to go out, so how do you feel about joining us?"

"Sounds like a plan," she said. "What time are you thinking?"

"I've heard there's a nice happy hour in Del Mar with a band playing and dancing. They start at six. What do you think?"

"Okay," she said. "I have a lot to catch up on today, so I'll connect with you around five? Sound good?"

"That's perfect," I replied, realizing this would give me all day to prepare for my first night out on the town. Suddenly, I was more than ready.

We arrived at the restaurant promptly at the start of happy hour and right away found an empty spot at a stand-up table, sharing it with a group already there. A rock band was playing, and the vibe was positive. I felt more alive than I'd felt in quite a while and psyched up to move forward and see what might be next. Who knows, maybe I'll meet a new prince, I chuckled silently.

However, as I sat there, I suddenly thought, "What am I doing here?" A wave of panic came over me but abruptly disappeared when one of the guys standing nearest us at our table introduced himself. He said that he and his buddies had just finished a 10K race. We smiled at his friends and raised our glasses to toast them.

Guy seemed friendly enough, and I could tell he was interested in finding out who of us was available.

"Would you like to dance?" he said, looking right at me.

"Sure," I smiled and followed him to the dance floor. It was a fast song, so I made eye contact and shyly shot him an occasional grin as we boogied to the music. As awkward as that was, I tried hard to relax and enjoy it. Next came a slow song, and he looked at me with his head cocked in question, eyebrows raised, so I moved in closer. When he put his hand on the small of my back, my entire body felt tingly. I secretly smiled to myself. Yes, I was still alive.

After a few more dances we returned to the table, where I realized that Cindy and Jim were ready to leave—they had two little ones waiting at home. So we said our goodbyes and left.

But when we were all seated in their car, I exclaimed, in a small voice from the back seat, "I don't think I'm ready to leave."

At that moment, without a word, everyone unbuckled, reached for their door handle, and together we walked back into the restaurant. They were aligned and clearly on board with me, making sure I was discovering what was next for me. They were all hoping something good would come my way. I was fortunate to have a family like that—they cared about me then and still do to this day.

As I walked through the door, Guy made a beeline toward me, smiled, and said, "I thought you were leaving?"

"We decided to stay for one more set," I smiled back. He gently took my hand and guided me to the dance floor. Giddy with excitement, I realized I hadn't felt this way in quite a long time. To say I was disappointed that he didn't ask for my number that night was an understatement. But I promptly turned it into a positive by reminding myself it was a huge miracle that I could feel that magical feeling again. And for that, I was thankful. I was slowly coming back to life.

The next weekend Sandy and I returned to the cafe in Del Mar, and Guy was there again, too. After a couple of dances, I noticed him walking over toward me. Once again, we danced the night away, and this time, as he walked me to my car, he asked if he could see me again. I was ecstatic and felt it was meant to be that we ran into each other again.

On Monday evening, he called me, and we enjoyed a nice chat. When our conversation was about to end, he asked if I'd like to join him on a hike the following Sunday. I gladly accepted and we had a wonderful day together.

We dated frequently after that, and by Thanksgiving we both were saying, "I love you." As we got to know one another, I realized he shared my desire to get married and have a family, and the love I was feeling for him was surprisingly similar to the love I initially felt for Bob. The following spring, he asked me to marry him, and we planned our wedding for September, one year after the day we met.

The night before our big day, we had the rehearsal and a dinner afterward hosted by Cindy and Jim. Esther surprised us and flew down from Seattle. Cheryl and Brian were there, also, along with our families and many friends.

A couple of months before our wedding day, I was finally purging the rest of Bob's clothes and personal items that I knew I needed to give away. I had hand-picked certain things for our loved ones to have as keepsakes, but it felt like it was now time to let go of the rest. Jim's mother, Wilma, knew of a church group that collected used clothes, and she was happy to take them from me to donate.

As I walked up to Cindy and Jim's house the night before my wedding, Wilma, who arrived at the same time, came up to me with a big smile.

"I went through all of the pockets of Bob's clothes before giving them away, Linda, and look what I found!"

She held up his original gold wedding ring, engraved inside with 'Bob~I love you~Linda 06-21-75,' which she told me she had found in one of the pockets of his jeans. It hadn't slipped off and in the ocean after all; it was here now and safe in my hands. Chills of joy spilled through my body as I hugged Wilma and thanked her for finding it. And, as I did, I looked up to the heavens. Was this a sign to me that I was doing the right thing?

Struggling internally, I am pretty sure I felt, or desperately wanted to feel, God and Bob smiling down on me while I recalled what Bob had told me just weeks before he died:

"I hope you will one day meet someone who loves you as much as I do, Linda, and that you will marry again."

Me too, I silently wondered to myself. I had recently been having doubts about my upcoming marriage, but hoped I had just received a message from above. I was to walk down the aisle the next day, and I prayed I was making the right decision.

As it turned out, God blessed our fifteen-year union with three beautiful, amazing children, and my dreams of becoming a mother finally came to fruition. Unfortunately, the marriage did not work out—and once again, I wondered about my happily ever after.

Through it all, however, I remained hopeful for my future.

CHAPTER FIFTEEN

What We Learned from Bob

THOUGH OUR TIME WITH each other was short, Bob and I jammed a lifetime into our nine years together, and we lived life. Never in my young mind did I imagine I would be a widow at the age of twenty-seven. Nor did I think I would end up childless and all alone, following a fabulous marriage and storybook love affair with the man of my dreams. That was not the promise in the fairy tales of my youth and not the happily ever after I had hoped for.

But come to find out, Bob was not mine to keep forever. He was a gift, and like everything in life, temporary. The Lord gives, and the Lord takes away. Possessions, family and friends, health, abilities, and time are all gifts from God. Through Bob, I learned not to back down, give up, or give in to my challenges, but rather to meet them head on and do my best to endure. He modeled how to face battles with dignity, grace, and faith. I realized that life is short and full of positive and disappointing changes.

To this day, I and many others follow his wise approach to life, to humbly make the most of the gifts we receive, help others in the meantime, and live each day to the fullest.

Although his time here on this earth was only twenty-six years and not the happily ever after he expected, his tsunami is long over. He made it through the storms, and how he lived it impacted those who were fortunate enough to know him. Ultimately, his life made a difference in how they have taken on their life storms.

Our amazing cousins, Cindy and Jim, who were with us through the entire cancer journey and well after, shared what they learned from Bob:

"As we look back, we think of our experience as a journey that Bob was leading.

In the end, he had to go away, but he left us all with the lessons he had taught us: To stay positive. To never lose your sense of humor. To appreciate each day and the people in your life. To never lose faith in God. To die with grace and dignity."

What a wonderful affirmation and tribute to an amazing man that was. If he were here to receive it, he would humbly smile and say, "Thank you. I appreciate hearing that. I'm just doing the best I can with what I have to work with." He would never take those words for granted.

During Bob's last year of life, Cindy and Jim were pregnant with their second baby. He was due to be born in October of 1981. Their first child, Katrina, was born six months before Bob's diagnosis in January 1979. These two babies were important to me, not just because they were my little cousins, but because they gave me a new purpose and a focus beyond the great tragedy in my life. Ultimately, they provided joy and hope for the present and the future.

In July of 1981, when Bob's body began to shut down, Cindy and Jim were with me most of the time, along with many other family members and friends. No doubt, this was a very stressful period for everyone, but a meaningful time, as well.

Our newest cousin and namesake, Robert, came in October, about nine weeks after Bob died from colon cancer. Immediately after his birth, little Rob had to undergo emergency surgery to repair a disconnection in his colon, which fortunately healed nicely. We later learned that the colon was forming while in utero during the time Bob was slowly slipping away, and my cousin Cindy was obviously, unavoidably emotionally stressed during her pregnancy.

That was a sign to me, once again, that there is something to this faith thing. Because to me, that was not a coincidence. And I would be remiss if I did not share what has worked for me, then and now; that in my mind, there is a higher power, reigning above all of us who think we are in control of this life. Far too many times, when I've been overwhelmed with decisions and situations and finally turned them over to God, he did not give up on me. Instead, I felt his presence center and guide me, so how can I help but believe and trust?

One might think that with all of the terrible and sad experiences I had during my time with Bob, I would become angry with God and give up on him. After all, what kind of God would do that, allow that to happen? Yes, I sometimes had these thoughts and wondered more than once "why me?" while left feeling confused and disappointed. However, amazingly, my faith has grown stronger and deeper as a result of my trials, and I choose to believe that since God has Bob and many other of my loved ones in his hands, which is where I ultimately hope to end up as well, I would be foolish to doubt. I have had too many signs that God is watching out for me, and I ultimately trust him with all my heart. Besides, grieving is so wonderfully different when you have the hope of eternity.

And since it takes nine months to come into this life, I do not believe that the spirit leaves this earth the moment one dies. Thus I constantly felt, and still feel, Bob's presence around me in various ways.

A few days after his passing, Bob visited me in our bedroom. He appeared as a vision I will never forget. Illuminated like a bright light, I saw him sitting at the foot of our bed, gazing at me, lying on his side of our king-size bed. He didn't come over to be near me; it was as if he wanted to stay for a moment to reassure me and let me know he was okay. I assumed he didn't want to give me false hope that he was back to stay.

That encounter provided much comfort, whether it was real or a dream. I felt peace knowing that Bob was safe where he was. I also knew he was looking out for me. I thanked God for allowing me to have that experience along with many others that have occurred since. God continues to give me glimpses of Bob through music, dreams, and other means, providing peace and assurance of my faith.

I miss Bob daily, and there is no doubt I always will. But instead of getting over him, I have learned how to navigate life without him tangibly being here. I also realize I am still here for a purpose. For how long, I have no idea, nor do I know what my future holds this side of heaven. But I am never alone. God is always with me, gently guiding and loving me. And since I can no longer take hold of Bob's hand, I've found comfort and strength in reaching up for God's hand instead. That, in itself, gives me hope!

* * *

Never Let Go of Hope

One day you will see
that it all has finally come together.
What you have always wished for
has finally come to be.

You will look back
and laugh at what has passed
and you will ask yourself,
"How did I get through all of that?"

Just never let go of hope.
Just never quit dreaming.
And never let love
depart from your life.

~jancarl campi

CHAPTER SIXTEEN

How God Used My Experiences for Good

I N RETROSPECT, OVER FORTY years after Bob passed, I can reflect on how that seemingly short period of my life with him affected my future. Watching Bob die at such a young age impacted the rest of my life. I learned early on how fragile life is and that it can be gone in a moment. As a result, I have lived life with passion, purpose, and meaning, trying hard not to let the moments slip through my fingers.

Relationships with others are so important to me, and I nurture them regularly. Paying close attention to who comes into my life and how we could affect one another, I have always looked for the reason or the purpose. I made a conscious effort never to take a day or an opportunity for granted. When I felt led to call or go to someone, I could not ignore the prompting. There was usually something good and meaningful that came from it. Whenever I heard a small voice telling me to contact a specific friend or family member, it often turned out they were in the midst of a crisis but too numb or weak to reach out for help. Those encounters encouraged me to be more attentive to my inner voice and gut feelings.

Having made it through my grief, I have a strong desire and urgency to use my experiences to help others, especially young widows and widowers. As a young mom, I had my hands full with caring for my little ones, but I always seemed drawn to someone who had recently lost a spouse and needed encouragement to move forward. It was easy and natural for me to share my story and give them hope for their future. That, in turn, led to some public speaking and facilitating grief support groups. My heart was always happy when I could use the tragedy I endured with Bob to console and inspire others, thus turning my pain into purpose.

I will never forget one encounter that reminded me that God was ever-present. While attending a morning Bible study at my church, one of my friends requested prayer for her neighbor, Jaymie.

"Her husband, Mike, is in the ICU in the final stages of myelofibrosis, cancer of the bone marrow," she said. "He is thirty-five, and they have three young children, ages six, four, and eleven months. Jaymie needs prayer to cope with this tragic situation."

That struck a chord deep within me, and I made it my mission to pray for this woman and her family and to reach out to her. Since their street was on my jogging path, I wondered which house was hers. I felt it was too personal to ask my friend, so I prayed while I ran and asked God for guidance.

A month or so later, while taking my regular run, I turned down the block where Jaymie lived, and right there on the corner house was a banner across the garage, thanking everyone for their prayers and support. My heart skipped a beat as I realized I had found her, but then I fell into sadness as I further read the message and saw that her husband, Mike, had moved on to heaven. I paused to pray for Jaymie and her family while I made a mental note of her address.

When I arrived home, I sat down and wrote a card to Jaymie explaining that although we didn't know each other, I understood the pain of loss. In it, I expressed my sadness for her and encouraged her to contact me if she ever felt like talking. It was a bold move, but I felt compelled in a way I could not ignore. I recognized I had a strong desire to minister to others experiencing similar devastating circumstances.

It was no surprise that Jaymie did not contact me. I decided to give her some time and had a feeling that one day we would connect when the timing was right. A couple of months later, following a prompting in my spirit, I looked up her phone number and left a voicemail letting her know she was not alone. I could not let it go.

One drizzly, cold evening several months later, I was on the baseball field with my two young daughters while we watched my son practice with his little league team. As we huddled together, hoping it would be over soon, I noticed another mom with her two young children and recognized that we were in the same boat.

"Hi," I smiled. "I hope this doesn't go much longer, don't you? It's freezing out here!"

She laughed and nodded her head.

"Looks like our kids are about the same age," I commented. "Mine are six, four, and eighteen months."

"Oh my gosh," she exclaimed. "My oldest out on the field is seven, but our younger ones are the same age. They keep us busy, right?"

"Oh yeah," I smiled. "Life is constant and always busy, but I love it."

"Me too," she grinned. But I sensed a sadness about her.

We continued to chat about the small stuff when, for some reason, she asked me if I belonged to a church, as she said she was looking for a new one in the area.

"I belong to a Presbyterian church nearby," I told her and mentioned the name.

"Oh, a friend on my street goes there, also, and she likes it a lot."

My eyes widened as I cocked my head and fixed my gaze on her.

"Are you Jaymie?"

She gave an instant look of confusion and then asked, "Yes. Are you Linda?"

"I am!"

We immediately hugged each other and looked up to the heavens.

"I have chills, Jaymie. I was not sure we would ever meet."

"Oh, I know. I kept meaning to contact you, but I just couldn't. You were so kind to reach out to me, but I wasn't ready, especially since I didn't even know you. And besides, I told myself I wasn't interested in talking to someone who was already remarried and moving forward. It was too much for me."

"Oh, I get it," I told her. We hugged again and assured each other we would stay in touch.

God brought me a special friend that night, and now, over thirty

Linda and Jaymie in recent years

years later, we are still the best of friends on a profound level. We have walked together through many trials since then. I am thankful I listened to that small voice I heard from above. Otherwise, I might have missed the gift.

Another poignant memory was the time I read in my local newspaper about a man, out jogging one morning, who was killed by a hit-and-run driver. The article mentioned the street he lived on, which was close to mine, and that he had left behind his newly wedded wife. My heart grieved for her—Nancy—and I felt compelled to find her. It was October, so a few days later, I picked up a little pumpkin, wrote her a card, and drove up and down the referenced street looking for clues.

Finally, amongst the many houses decorated for fall, I spotted a porch filled with floral arrangements and concluded that must be the one. I prayed as I knocked on the door, asking for God's guidance and words to speak. A lovely young woman meekly opened the door, her expression was puzzled. An older man stood behind her.

"Are you Nancy?" I asked.

"Yes, I am."

"Hi Nancy, I'm Linda. I live in the neighborhood and read about your husband," I gently explained. "I just wanted to offer you some comfort and support at this difficult time."

She invited me in and I handed her the card I'd written and the pumpkin.

"This is my dad," she said, her eyes welling with tears. "He's staying with me for a while so I'm not alone."

I told her I had been widowed at a young age and mentioned that if she ever wanted to talk, I'd be happy to meet with her. We exchanged numbers and I told her to feel free to call me anytime.

As I was leaving, she hugged me, while tears slid down her cheeks.

"We just moved here recently and I haven't made too many friends. I will call you for sure. Thank you for reaching out to me, Linda."

I sat in my car, collecting my thoughts. Thank you, God, I prayed. I would not have done this without your prompting.

Nancy contacted me a couple of weeks later and we began taking morning walks together after I took my children to school. She freely shared her thoughts, emotions, and fears as we moved through her grief. It was a win-win for both of us, as I, in helping her, realized how far I had come in my own healing. My youngest daughter also became quite fond of Nancy, and even shared her story in a first-grade poster project, which included the original newspaper article I had found.

Nancy plodded through her first year of widowhood and slowly began to make changes necessary to grow herself. I shared my formula for "creating a new me," while she worked hard to put the broken dreams back together and produce a fully revised blueprint for her life. Eventually, she relocated for a fresh start and, in doing so, met someone special. I was happy to share in her joy. Our time together was brief, but meaningful, and I will never forget it.

As my children grew older, I had a yearning to do more. As you may recall, Bob died the night before I was to contact hospice for help. I felt a strong calling that I needed to work with a hospice organization to further my outreach to those in need of comfort, compassion, and hope. In a leap of faith, I took a day off from work, made an appointment, and visited a hospice in my community. I met with two supervisors and told them my story about Bob and how I longed to share the benefits of hospice with others, those services that I wasn't fortunate enough to receive myself.

"I'm not sure how I landed here," I told them, "but I know I'm searching for my next rainbow."

They looked at each other and back at me and said, "We just had a meeting about that very position this morning and you would be the perfect candidate. I think you've found your rainbow!"

For the next five years, I met with countless families and their terminally-ill loved ones and helped them navigate and transition through some very sorrow-filled moments. I often shared my experience with others about how my situation would have been so much better and easier had I known about the benefits of this service before Bob came to the end of his journey. I continued to use Bob's life and death experience to provide comfort and hope, which also helped me feel like I was giving back to many in exchange for the priceless gift he was to me, keeping his memory alive.

I've learned that time is precious and not to be wasted. None of us know how long we have here on earth, so it makes sense to do our best to make the most of each day. This life can be difficult, and curve balls will come your way, but it's how you catch them and move forward that matters. That makes all the difference. God trusted me with this journey, and I intend to continue to live it to the fullest and do all I can with what I am given and have learned.

* * *

Ironically, forty-something years later, I reconnected with Bob's best friend, John, who is now a doctor and divorced with five grown children. He was with me when Bob died, and we are still best friends. Our emotional connection runs deep, and he knows me better than most.

I planned a visit to John and his family in North Carolina in June of my 60th year. Prior to my trip I had my annual physical/gynecological exam. While there, I strongly felt that I needed to advocate for myself and ask her for a more thorough pelvic assessment, even though I had no symptoms, just an overwhelming gut instinct. Because of my age, my doctor hesitated to acknowledge my request, but since I insisted, due to my history with Bob, she finally complied. She said she would send the specimen to pathology and also referred me to a gynecologist for a biopsy just to be sure. During the biopsy appointment, the doctor assured me it was probably nothing of concern. I was not the least bit worried and went forward with my trip to North Carolina.

As promised, John was curbside when I landed, waiting for me. He jumped out of the car and we hugged each other tightly. It felt so right being there with him after all these years.

Three hours after I landed in Raleigh, we were driving to get some lunch when my phone rang.

"I'd better take this call," I told John. Sure enough, it was my doctor in California who had performed the biopsy.

"I'm so sorry to tell you this, Linda, but I was wrong to minimize your concerns about your exam last week. The mass we tested is malignant." John could tell by my side of the conversation that something was wrong. He took my hand and gently squeezed it.

"*Malignant?*" I gasped. I had no words and suddenly my hearing stopped functioning. "I'm going to put you on speaker so my friend who is with me can listen also. Could you repeat what you just said?"

John pulled the car to the curb and took my phone. "You have Stage One adenocarcinoma," she repeated, "and we need to arrange for surgery right away. I am so sorry to have to tell you this. The surgeon will be calling you later today to make arrangements. This needs to be done sooner rather than later, Linda."

John asked a few more medical questions while I completely tuned out and went into my head, totally caught off guard. When the call ended, he turned to me, took my hand, and reassured me that, given the circumstances, I was most likely going to be okay. Thank God he was there.

But wait! What? How does this happen? I was just beginning a new chapter in my life, an exciting adventure. How does this even fit in? Way to screw up my plans, Doc. Additionally, John had previously invited me to go with him to his annual family reunion in the Outer Banks, so now I not only had to cut my trip short, but I also had to miss that trip due to a stupid cancer. This was not what I had planned, God.

My surgeon called me later that day and was as nice as could be.

"We are going to take good care of you, Linda, and put this behind us. I've scheduled your surgery for July 3, in the morning, but will need to see you next week for a pre-op visit. You can make an appointment for that when I connect you to our front desk."

The remainder of the week was spent just relaxing and spending time with John and his family, and I eventually shared this news with them, over pizza, attempting to keep it light and hopefully minimize my fear and angst. I didn't want them to worry. His sister Lisa will never let me forget how nonchalant I was!

It was so reassuring to share my feelings with John, as he was very positive after speaking with my doctor. But when the day came to say goodbye, I was incredibly sad.

"I feel like I should come to Cali and be there for you," John said while driving me to the airport.

"That's sweet of you, Johnny, but you need to be with your kids at the reunion. This will be a bonding time for all of you with your family, and you will be making some incredible memories, as well. I've already talked to several friends and my cousin who will be going with me. I'll be fine. I just want to get this behind me and move on with my life. I'll keep you posted—you go and enjoy. Just pray for me that it goes well."

"I'm so sorry this is happening for you, Linda, and I'm amazed at how well you are handling it, although that's not really a surprise. I think I'd be freaking out myself."

"Not much else I can do besides pray and go through it, right? I'm just so thankful you were with me when I got the news."

We hugged goodbye and he softly assured me he would be praying.

As I rolled my bag into the airport lobby, I turned around one more time to wave and blow him a kiss. It was hard to recall when I had felt this forlorn...and scared.

Linda and John—then and now

Walking slowly through the terminal, I literally dragged my feet through security and to my gate. When I finally plopped into my seat on the plane, I stared ahead and thought about the contrast of this flight versus the one last week. I went from total excitement to see John and his family for an extended vacation to an early departure to go home and take care of a cancer surgery. Such a strange turn of events. I looked around me and wondered what stories were tucked inside each passenger. It reminded me that not every trip was for pleasure.

When the day came for my pre-op appointment, I was accompanied by my friends, Cheryl and Wendy, and my cousin, Cindy. The doctor referred to them as my posse. He alleviated my fears with his amazing bedside manner and I felt comfortable in his care. The following week, my posse, which had now grown by two more dear friends, Jaymie and Riki, went with me for the all-day event.

The surgery itself went well and the initial biopsy showed no lymph node involvement, which was a relief. I stayed with my cousins for a couple of nights and then returned home and continued to recuperate while I waited to hear about the results of the pathology report.

I was enjoying a morning cup of coffee one week later when my surgeon called to ask how I was doing.

"I feel great," I said, inhaling a quick anxious breath.

"Well, you're going to be even better when we finish chatting. I just received the results of your final pathology report. There was no evidence of cancer spread."

Chills of relief spilled through my body and a big smile came over me, which I'm sure he sensed.

"Linda, you are as close to being 100% cancer-free as one can be, considering what you've experienced. And you will need no further treatment, no chemo, no radiation therapy. I'm so very happy for you."

This "clean" outcome was delivered four weeks from the day I received my initial diagnosis. To say I felt grateful is putting it mildly. I immediately contacted everyone who was there with me, and those who had been praying for me, and I excitedly shared the good news. I was cancer-free...a cancer survivor.

As I hung up the phone, a huge release came over me and I felt as though I'd been shot out of a cannon. A new breath of fresh air and sense of freedom engulfed me. I knew in my heart that it was time to do all that I had dreamed of. This had been a wake-up call, once again, of how fragile and short this life is. Suddenly, I realized that the sands of time in my own hourglass were slipping through quickly, and I felt an incredible desire to live life NOW.

Purging became my new pastime and soon my life was reduced down to a furnished condo, ready to rent, a five-by-seven foot storage unit for those items I couldn't quite part with, and a compact car filled with as many treasures as I felt I needed to begin my new life. I had lived my entire life in California and my dream was to live in a different state and experience the four seasons. What better choice than to live near my family in North Carolina? My goal was to leave in August, and it wasn't long before my condo was rented. I soon found myself pulling out of the driveway, heading east, right on schedule.

A twenty-five-hundred-mile road trip lay ahead of me, and I was as excited as a kid going to Disneyland for the first time. Setting out alone on this journey, with God as my co-pilot, there was no doubt or fear in my entire being about what I was doing. Snacks were packed, tunes were streaming, and beautiful scenery awaited my arrival. My heart was full of hope. Let the journey begin ... Mid-Life Crisis here I come!

So, at age sixty, I was diagnosed with the same type of fast-growing cancer my husband battled at twenty-four, only in a different part of my body. But because mine was detected early and at a much less advanced stage, it was treatable and curable. As a result of the plight Bob endured, I knew enough to speak up for myself and make sure I was doing all I could to take care of myself. I had learned much from my time with Bob about how to tackle a scary cancer diagnosis. I fell back on his bravery and positive attitude, most especially when I was being wheeled into the operating room. It felt like he was—and still is—walking me through my life journey.

All that to say, I learned to be more proactive and advocate for myself.

As a result, my life, for now, was spared. But who knows what tomorrow brings?

Since I watched my beloved Bob transition out of this life and into the next, I know in my heart that where he is now is where I want to end up also. If I am wrong, so be it, but if I am right, then hallelujah! In my mind, this life is not all there is. For me, there is hope, faith, and joy in each new day. And I pray that for each and every one of you.

"In My Mind I'm Going to Carolina!"

Epilogue

All of my life experiences now leave me to wonder what "happily ever after" really means. What does it look like? Do I have to have a partner to feel complete and successful? Does it need to include an altar relationship with a significant other? Maybe finding a handsome prince isn't the only answer to the fairytale life and happily ever after that was promised to me as a young girl.

My fairy-tale expectations assured me that my life would be labeled a failure if I didn't have a partner and a happy marriage. But I learned from experience that having a happy union with someone who wanted to be with me and work together along life's path as a team is a gift. Yet that gift can also be temporary.

Not long ago, I realized that not everyone needs a partner to feel happy and content. Having had my fair share of relationships has helped me see that the life God has mapped out for me is more than fulfilling. I have immersed myself in family and dear friends whom I love. They are there for me no matter what and mean just as much to me as finding a 'forever' relationship.

Of course, I miss the positive aspects of a loving, intimate partnership, but I have managed to create a meaningful life without that for now. And I say "for now" because I never know what's coming next. I've given it a good hard try and have consistently dated through each decade of my adult life since my first date at sixteen. I've had blind dates, met people at social gatherings, and joined several online dating sites, but so far, I've been unsuccessful in meeting anyone I wanted to sail with for the rest of my life.

Now, well into my sixties, I finally realize I have come full circle from my short fairy-tale life with Bob. Although I loved being married and am thankful for what I had with him, I am now complete as a single woman and honestly have all I could ever want. I value my independence and freedom to do what I please, to choose who I want in my life, to go where I want, and to devote my time to others whenever and wherever I can. I'm free to follow my heart. And I've realized that my life, as it is, is a true "happily ever after." I am content, and that, in itself, is a happy place to be.

Linda's Family 2023

My three beautiful children have grown into wonderful, capable, productive adults who all are successful on their own. They have found their significant others and have loving, nurturing relationships. I enjoy spending time with them and love who they have become.

Recently, I became a Nana and am the primary 'Nanny' for my little grandson and two granddaughters. What a joy to be a part of their lives and spend my days watching them grow and develop. It's a gift I could never have imagined would be so wonderfully fulfilling. They captured my heart from day one.

Nana with Ryan, Coco and Romy

Lastly, I want to mention the joy and companionship my granddogs bring to my life. I often have the privilege of doggie-sitting, and the unconditional love of these sweet pets has added greatly to my contentment.

Kowalski and Georgia   *Pebbles and Cholula*

"Happily ever after" is just that. It's not the means to an end. It is about enjoying every moment, and feeling content, wherever you are in life, for as long as it lasts. I will never get over Bob or stop loving and missing him. He is fully alive and present in my heart as a sweet memory and precious time of my life. But I've learned how to live my life without him.

My hope and prayer in writing this memoir is that it will bring hope and healing to anyone possibly walking a similar journey.

"As every thread of gold is valuable, so is every moment of time."
~John Mason

It's In The Valleys I Grow

Sometimes life seems hard to bear,
Full of sorrow, trouble, and woe.
It's then I have to remember
That it's in the valleys I grow.

If I always stayed on the mountaintop
And never experienced pain,
I would never appreciate God's love
And would be living in vain.

I have so much to learn
And my growth is very slow.
Sometimes I need the mountaintops,
But it's in the valleys I grow.

I do not always understand
Why things happen as they do,
But I am very sure of one thing.
My Lord will see me through.

My little valleys are nothing
When I picture Christ on the cross.
He went through the valley of death;
His victory was Satan's loss.

Forgive me Lord, for complaining
When I'm feeling so very low.
Just give me a gentle reminder
That it's in the valleys I grow.

Continue to strengthen me, Lord
And use my life each day
To share your love with others
And help them find their way.

Thank you for valleys, Lord
For this one thing I know;
The mountaintops are glorious
But it's in the valleys I grow!

By Janet Eggleston

Acknowledgments

A special thank you to everyone who ultimately had a hand in the birth of my memoir, following a more than ten-year labor of love; those of you who cheered me on to the completion of this goal—you know who you are. Thank you for your part in bringing this book to life.

To Bob, without whom this book would not exist. You, my love, gave me not only your heart, but your soul, and I thank you. You were, and still are, my eternal soulmate.

Those with us on the journey:

My family - My sister, Sandy Anderson; my cousins, Cindy and Jim Crew, Rick Biggs; my parents, Bill and LorEtta Schroder; my aunt and uncle, Dick and Juanita Biggs; my grandma and grandpa, Memoo and Papa Lee, all of whom supported me and rarely left my side.

Our lifelong friends - Rocky and Esther Smith, John and Chris Gentri, Cheryl and Brian Hatkoff, Rocky Pangallo, Marty Goehner. Thank you for always, and still, being there for me.

Dr. Philip Brooks, MD, Obstetrics and Gynecology, for his caring, hopeful, and determined efforts in counseling Bob and me in our infertility challenge.

Those with me on the journey of creating and launching my book:

Eva Shaw - Author, mentor, and instructor of my first online class, Write Your Life Story, where she nudged me to "keep writing—you have an important story to tell."

Fern Field Brooks - Author, friend, and mentor who graciously critiqued my writing and again and again inspired me to continue on.

Temecula West Writers Guild - Jeff, John, Chris, Luke, Lori, Mary, Michelle, Theresa, Heidi, and Eliot. I'm ever grateful for the spot-on critiques from this group, which provided a springboard for me in my writing skills. Thank you for your encouragement to finish this project. And special thanks to my son, Kevin, for planting a seed that I might want to join a writers group. Best thing I could have done!

Nancy Feraco - My dear friend and cheerleader who read numerous excerpts before I submitted them for critique and offered suggestions that ultimately improved my ability to "show and not tell" my story.

Cindy Crew - My cousin and my anchor, who has known me longer than anyone, and is always there to encourage, support, and help me, especially when I can't find the right words.

Evelyn Huey - My dear friend and adopted "mom" who has always supported and encouraged me in everything I do—especially while writing this book.

Special thanks to those who read the entire rough draft of my manuscript and offered valuable feedback, praise, and encouragement - Marilyn Jasco, Diane McCloskey, John Gentri, and Claire Winchester.

Holli Hiddessen - My amazing editor and friend who had the patience of a saint while we cherry-picked words and phrases and who helped calm and center me when I worried I was omitting something or someone. She has read my book numerous times, and each time has come back with applause. Thank you, Holli, for coming alongside me on this journey and pulling me "out of the weeds" when necessary, encouraging me to finish and hopefully make a difference.

Jeff Waddleton - Writing class instructor and mentor, who has continually nudged me to finish my story, reminding me how much it could help others, and who invited me to join the Temecula West Writers Guild. Jeff also created the most incredible cover for my book—I cried when I first saw it—and creatively formatted my story into a real book. He had unbelievable patience, hanging in there through my countless edits while I continued to strive for perfection. Thank you, Jeff, for turning this dream of mine into a reality.

Katrina Crew - My cousin, published author, and encourager. Thank you for always being available to edit, inspire, and enlighten me on the world of self-publishing. You mapped out the way for me to move forward and I am forever grateful.

Kevin & Jaki, Amy & Eric, Laura & Jamie - My precious children. You are gifts from God. Thank you for the joy you bring to my life.

* * *

I never realized how challenging yet rewarding and cathartic it could be to write a personal story from the heart. Above all, I want to thank God for being ever-present in my life. I wouldn't have endured and recovered from this real life experience, much less write about it, without God as my guide.

www.ingramcontent.com/pod-product-compliance
Lightning Source LLC
Chambersburg PA
CBHW020242130626
46549CB00005B/2020